ELISABETH PRESCHER

ENGLISH COMPACT GRAMMAR

A to Z

GRAMÁTICA COMPACTA DA
LÍNGUA INGLESA
COM EXERCÍCIOS E RESPOSTAS

2ª reimpressão

© 2014 Elisabeth Prescher

Preparação de texto
Larissa Lino Barbosa/Verba Editorial

Capa e projeto gráfico
Paula Astiz

Editoração eletrônica
Laura Lotufo/Paula Astiz Design

Revisão
Albina Escobar

Assistente editorial
Aline Naomi Sassaki

Dados Internacionais de Catalogação na Publicação (CIP)
(Câmara Brasileira do Livro, SP, Brasil)

Prescher, Elisabeth
   English compact grammar : A to Z / Elisabeth Prescher.
— Barueri, SP : DISAL, 2014.

   ISBN 978-85-7844-167-8

   1. Inglês – Estudo e ensino 2. Inglês – Gramática I. Título.

14-09505   CDD-420.7

Índices para catálogo sistemático:
1. Inglês : Gramática : Linguística : Estudo e ensino 420.7

Todos os direitos reservados em nome de:
Bantim, Canato e Guazzelli Editora Ltda.

Alameda Mamoré 911 – cj. 107
Alphaville – BARUERI – SP
CEP: 06454-040
Tel./Fax: (11) 4195-2811
Visite nosso site: www.disaleditora.com.br
Televendas: (11) 3226-3111

Fax gratuito: 0800 7707 105/106
e-mail para pedidos: comercialdisal@disal.com.br

Nenhuma parte desta publicação pode ser reproduzida, arquivada ou transmitida de nenhuma forma ou meio sem permissão expressa e por escrito da Editora.

Contents

A

1. Abstract Nouns I: characteristics — 9
2. Abstract Nouns II: form — 11
3. Adjectives I: use — 13
4. Adjectives II: form — 15
5. Adjectives III: order — 17
6. Adverbs I: use — 19
7. Adverbs II: form & spelling — 21
8. Adverbs III: position — 23
9. Adverbs IV: order — 25
10. Adverb or Adjective? — 27
11. Adverb List: manner, place, time — 29
12. Agreement: subject & verb — 31
13. Articles: indefinite and definite — 33
14. Auxiliary & Modal Verbs — 35

B

15. Basic Sentence Patterns — 37
16. Be: present & past — 39

C

17. Collective & Compound Nouns — 41
18. Conditional Sentences I: use — 43
19. Conditional Sentences II: verb tenses — 45
20. Conjunctions I: list — 47
21. Conjunctions II: list — 49
22. Countable & Uncountable Nouns — 51

D

23.	Degrees of Comparison I: more/most ..., ...-er/-est	53
24.	Degrees of Comparison II: irregular comparison	55
25.	Demonstratives & Distributives: this, that etc	57
26.	Do: present & past	59
27.	Do & Make	61

E

28.	Exclamatory Sentences & Other Sentence Types	63

F

29.	Future Tenses I: general table	65
30.	Future Tenses II: future simple & going to	67
31.	Future Tenses III: future progressive & future perfect	69

G

32.	Gender of Nouns	71
33.	Gerund I: Gerund & Present Participle	73
34.	Gerund II: verbs followed by Gerund or Infinitive	75

H

35.	Have I: present & past	77
36.	Have II: causative form	79
37.	How & Compounds	81

I

38.	Imperative	83
39.	Indefinites I: some, any, no, none	85
40.	Indefinites II: compounds	87
41.	Infinitive I: characteristics	89
42.	Infinitive II: infinitive with to – list	91

L

43.	Linking Verbs	93

M

44.	Modal Auxiliaries I: characteristics	95
45.	Modal Auxiliaries II: meaning	97
46.	Mood	99

N

47.	Nouns I: characteristics	101
48.	Nouns II: form	103
49.	Numerals: cardinal & ordinal numbers – list	105

O

50.	One	107
51.	Ordinary Verbs	109

P

52.	Participles: present & past	111
53.	Passive Voice	113
54.	Past Tenses I: general table	115
55.	Past Tenses II: past progressive	117
56.	Past Tenses III: past simple – regular verbs	119
57.	Past Tenses IV: past simple – irregular verbs	121
58.	Past Tenses V: past perfect & past perfect progressive	123
59.	Personal Pronouns: subject & object	125
60.	Phrasal Verbs: list	127
61.	Plural of Nouns: regular & irregular	129
62.	Possessive Adjectives & Pronouns	131
63.	Possessive of Nouns ('s or ')	133
64.	Prefixes and Suffixes	135
65.	Prepositions	137
66.	Preposition Combinations: prepositions after verbs	139
67.	Present Tenses I: general table	141
68.	Present Tenses II: present progressive	143
69.	Present Tenses III: present simple	145
70.	Present Tenses IV: present perfect x past simple	147
71.	Present Tenses V: present perfect & present perfect progressive	149

Q

72.	Quantifiers: much, many etc.	151
73.	Questions: direct & indirect (embedded)	153

R

74.	Reflexive Pronouns	155
75.	Relative Pronouns I: who, which, that etc.	157
76.	Relative Pronouns II: relative clauses	159
77.	Reported Speech	161

S

| 78. | Spelling & Pronunciation: final s/es, d/ed, er/est, ing | 163 |

T

| 79. | Tag Question | 165 |
| 80. | There To Be: present & past | 167 |

V

| 81. | Verb Tense Table | 169 |

W

| 82. | Wh-questions | 171 |

X

| 83. | X-doubts: also, too, either; each other, one another; enough; inversion; it takes; like, as; so … I, neither … I; whom; would rather, had better; yet, already, still | 173 |

Y

| 84. | Yes-no Questions | 175 |

85. **Zero Article** 177

Answers 179

Irregular Verbs 217

1 Abstract Nouns I

Characteristics

Substantivos abstratos fazem referência a tudo que não pode ser percebido ou experimentado pelos sentidos. Nomeiam estados, atributos, acontecimentos, movimentos, ideias, conceitos, emoções, sentimentos etc.:

pain   beauty   progress   socialism   death   love   hunger

Substantivos abstratos podem ser contáveis como **dream/s** e **problem/s** ou incontáveis como **faith** e **patriotism**.

states, attributes	ideas, ideals, concepts
beauty, brilliance, compassion, loyalty, misery, pain, skill, success	beliefs, culture, dedication, dreams, faith, information, knowledge, liberty
events, movements	**emotions, feelings**
education, friendship, hospitality, leisure, progress, relaxation, trouble	anger, hate, peace, pride, sympathy, hatred

Exercises [answers on p. 179]

1 Check the correct synonyms for the abstract nouns below.

1. kindness   a. friendship   b. goodness ✓   c. lovely
2. courage   a. cowardice   b. dedication   c. bravery
3. importance a. weakness   b. relevance   c. difference
4. friendship a. companionship   b. antagonism   c. hate
5. despair   a. hopelessness   b. ambition   c. hope
6. happiness   a. misery   b. satisfaction c. sadness
7. prosperity a. success   b. poverty   c. bad luck
8. adversity   a. fortune   b. misfortune   c. approval
9. faith   a. confidence   b. infidelity   c. doubt
10. leisure   a. relaxation   b. work   c. information

2 Underline the correct words to complete the sentences.

1. He couldn't hide his (pride – proud) for his players.
2. She shows great (affection – affect) for her students.
3. You have to respect the (lovely – love) she has for her baby.
4. The child looked at the cake with (satisfy – satisfaction).
5. His eyes were full of (hope – hopeless) when he entered the office.
6. Each one takes his own (decide – decisions).
7. He who sleeps forgets (hungry – hunger).
8. They showed extreme (joy – joyful) when they helped us.
9. He said he was fighting for (freedom – free).
10. She was admired for her (courageous – courage).
11. (Time – timely) is a great teacher.
12. (Creativity – Create) allows us to make (mistakes – bridges).

3 Underline the abstract nouns in each sentence.

1. Always tell the truth.
2. Honesty is the best policy.
3. Everybody admired her beauty.
4. Don't treat animals with cruelty.
5. They didn't take my advice seriously.
6. I have an idea to solve the problem.
7. Those men were arrested for disturbing the peace.
8. Her hatred towards her classmates is obvious.
9. Never tell a lie.
10. The soldier was hurt and cried in pain.
11. Adversity introduces a man to himself.
12. Do the workers believe in justice?

2 Abstract Nouns II

Form

Alguns **substantivos abstratos** como *love, peace, hope, joy* etc. têm forma própria. Outros podem ser formados acrescentando-se prefixos e sufixos a adjetivos, verbos ou a outros substantivos.

prudent → **im**prud**ence**
(adj.)

act → **in**act**ion**
(v.)

child → child**hood**
(subst.)

sufixos mais usados	prefixos mais usados
-ability: prob**ability**	**dis-: dis**advantage
-acy: conspir**acy**	**in-: in**convenience
-ance/-ence: prud**ence**	**mal-: mal**function
-ism: favorit**ism**	**mis-: mis**take
-ity, -y: stupid**ity**, honest**y**	**un-: un**happiness
-ment: content**ment**	
-ness: tired**ness**	
-ship: friend**ship**	
-tion: adora**tion**	

Exercises [answers on p. 179]

1 Underline the suffixes in the abstract nouns below.

1. affec<u>tion</u>
2. agreement
3. ambition
4. brutality
5. carelessness
6. cheerfulness
7. communication
8. confidence
9. creation
10. curiosity
11. dedication
12. dictatorship
13. disappointment
14. disturbance
15. eagerness

2 Underline the prefixes in the abstract nouns below.

1. <u>dis</u>appointment
2. unbalance
3. informality
4. miscalculation
5. inutility
6. disapproval
7. unfair
8. misdirection
9. malnutrition

10. misfortune
11. unhappiness
12. disadvantage
13. disbelief
14. indifference
15. maladministration

3 Choose the correct form of the corresponding abstract noun.

1. adjust: a. justify b. maladjustment ✓
2. connect: a. connected b. misconnection
3. qualify: a. equal b. qualification
4. refresh: a. fresh b. refreshment
5. safe: a. safety b. unsafe
6. tired: a. tiredly b. tiredness
7. ugly: a. ugliness b. ugliest
8. weak: a. weakness b. weekly
9. comfort: a. discomfort b. comfortably
10. national: a. nationally b. nationalism

4 Turn the words into abstract nouns. Use suffixes or prefixes.

suffixes: -ability -acy -ance/-ence -ism -ity -y -ment -ness -ship -tion
prefixes: dis- in- mal- mis- un-

1. enjoy — *enjoyment*
2. fascinate
3. favorite
4. formal
5. friend
6. glad
7. happy
8. hero
9. imagine
10. move
11. patriot
12. organize

3 Adjectives I

Use

Adjetivos são palavras como *tall, short, big* e *small*. São usados para descrever pessoas, coisas ou animais. Têm uma única forma que pode ser usada tanto para o masculino e feminino quanto para o singular e plural.

happy boy   **happy** girl   **happy** children

Adjetivos são usados...

1. antes de substantivos:	2. após verbos de ligação:
They have **beautiful** children.	This book is **interesting**.
The **red** book is mine.	You look **tired**.

Note – Verbos de ligação: appear, be, become, feel, get, look, make, seem, smell, sound, taste.

Exercises [answers on p. 180]

1 Check the opposites of the underlined adjectives.

1. They like to live in <u>big</u> houses.
   a. pretty   b. old   c. small ✓
2. She has <u>an expensive</u> new coat.
   a. a cheap   b. a long   c. an interesting
3. He is <u>a handsome</u> pilot.
   a. an ugly   b. an angry   c. a short
4. We had many <u>cold</u> days last winter.
   a. cloudy   b. agreeable   c. hot
5. Karl is <u>a sad</u> little boy.
   a. a tall   b. an unhappy   c. a happy
6. She told me this is <u>a dangerous</u> place.
   a. an ugly   b. a safe   c. a narrow
7. The coffee is <u>cold</u>. Let me prepare some fresh one.
   a. ugly   b. sweet   c. hot

8. Jorge likes fast cars.
   a. quick   b. slow   c. new
9. The wolf had long teeth.
   a. short   b. thin   c. thick
10. They don't know the right answer.
    a. correct   b. wrong   quiet

2 Circle the correct adjective.

1. The pirate had long (black – cheap) hair.
2. Carol seems (modern – happy) today. Is it her birthday?
3. Grandpa knows many (expensive – interesting) stories.
4. The wind became (tired – strong).
5. Those kids are very (intelligent – noisy). They get good grades.
6. Do you live in that (young – old), white house?
7. The mangoes taste (good – yellow).
8. She bought pretty, new, (yellow – round) shoes.
9. It is autumn. The leaves turned (cold – red).
10. He made a big, (blue and yellow – sad) kite.

3 Complete the sentences with the words in the box.

| difficult   interesting   careful   delicious |
| horrible   young   new   Old   brave   good |

1. I asked him an _____interesting_____ question.
2. They found the exercise _____.
3. You car looks _____.
4. My sister is a very _____ girl.
5. He wrote a book called "The _____ Man and the Sea".
6. The _____ man saved the girl from the fire.
7. Don't worry. He is a _____ driver.
8. He is a _____ singer. You should watch his show.
9. The food is _____ here. Let's go to another restaurant.
10. This cake tastes _____. I love it!

4 Adjectives II

Form

Alguns **adjetivos** como *beautiful, uncertain, helpless* e *golden* são formados a partir de outras palavras.

É possível formar adjetivos...

1. pelo acréscimo de sufixos:	2. pelo acréscimo de prefixos:
-ed: interest**ed** **-ing:** fascinat**ing** **-y:** cloud**y** **-ful:** care**ful** **-less:** care**less** **-ish:** child**ish** **-able:** wash**able** etc.	**dis-:** **dis**content **in-:** **in**correct **super-:** **super**ego etc.
	3. pela junção de palavras: dark-blue blue-eyed good-looking old-fashioned etc.

Exercises [answers on p. 180]

1 Underline the correct words to complete the sentences.

1. It is a (<u>long</u> – length) way to his house.
2. The girls were (frighten – frightened) because they had seen a mouse.
3. A race for horses is a (horse race – race horse).
4. We were (powerful – powerless). We could do nothing to help.
5. I get (boring – bored) when I go to formal events.
6. A story about love is a (love story – story love).
7. A dog that behaves well is a (well-behaved – behaved well) dog.
8. A dress for a wedding is a (dress wedding – wedding dress).
9. Something that is not possible is (improbable – impossible).
10. She is (interesting – interested) in Roman architecture.

2. Turn the words below into adjectives. Use suffixes.

| -ed | -ing | -y | -ful | -less | -ish | -able |

1. anger — *angry*
2. beauty —
3. child —
4. color —
5. disappoint —
6. disgust —
7. drink —
8. ease —
9. excite —
10. fascinate —
11. fool —
12. happiness —
13. home —
14. hope —
15. juice —
16. luck —
17. misery —
18. pain —
19. question —
20. ugliness —

5 Adjectives III

Order

Adjetivos em série são usados em ordem específica, não aleatória.

I love that **pretty**, **old**, **round**, **brown** table.
(opinião) (idade) (forma) (cor)

Embora não seja aconselhável o uso de muitos adjetivos juntos, a tabela traz a ordem em que os diferentes tipos de adjetivos devem ser colocados. Observe:

The first two **good big old square brown known Chinese stone religious** temples were built a long time ago.

determiner[1]/adjective	example	sentence
1. articles, possessives, etc.	the, a, this, my...	The
2. ordinal number	first, second...	first
3. quantity	two, much, some...	two
4. opinion, description[2]	good, bad...	**good**
5. size, height, length	big, small...	**big**
6. age, temperature	old, hot...	**old**
7. shape	round, square...	**square**
8. color	blue, brown...	**brown**
9. participle	known, amazing...	**known**
10. origin, location	Asian, Chinese...	**Chinese**
11. material	rock, wooden...	**stone**
12. purpose	sleeping, frying...	**religious temples...**

Notes – (1) determiners são palavras que vêm junto a substantivos: demonstrativos, artigos, possessivos, numerais etc. A maioria dos determiners é classificada como adjetivo.
(2) adjetivos do mesmo tipo: use a ordem que preferir. Ex: I have a gentle, kind, funny son. (opinion)

Exercises [answers on p. 181]

1 Underline the correct order.

1. My mother lives in a (<u>small white</u> – white small) house.
2. I want to buy those (five good – good five) books.
3. Charles is (an old traveling – a traveling old) salesman.
4. I hate the (cold first – first cold) days of winter.
5. He got better during the (two last – last two) months.
6. They are going to destroy those (dilapidated old brick – old dilapidated brick) houses.
7. I have lost my (dark brown, small – small, dark brown) leather case.
8. There are (three empty – empty three) houses in our street.
9. My husband is (a dark-haired, big – a big, dark-haired) man.

2 Underline the correct order.

1. She wants to become (a singing international – <u>an international singing</u>) star.
2. We use (fresh British – British fresh) ingredients.
3. Her neighbor is (an old, interesting – an interesting, old) Dutch man.
4. He drives (a big, expensive – an expensive, big) German car.
5. I love (fine, old – old, fine) Spanish wine.
6. We saw (a brick old white – an old white brick) house.
7. We gave him (a wonderful old Italian – an old wonderful Italian) clock.
8. The (black, old, big – big, old, black) dog slept under the couch.
9. Archeologists have found (large, prehistoric – prehistoric, large) animal bones.

6 Adverbs I

Order

Advérbios são palavras como *slowly, here, now, often, perhaps* etc.

Fornecem informações sobre verbos, adjetivos, outros advérbios ou frases inteiras. Advérbios informam *quando, onde, como* ou *por que* algo acontece. É bom lembrar que adjetivos descrevem substantivos (pessoa, coisa ou animal).

Dad *drives* **slowly**.
He drives **very** *fast*.

I bought a **very** *good* car.
Yesterday, *I watched a great match*.

manner:	**frequency:**
slowly, quickly, well etc.	often, seldom, never
He drives **slowly**.	She is **often** angry.
place:	**doubt/ degree:**
here, there, upstairs, at home	maybe, perhaps, so, too, very etc.
I live **upstairs**.	**Maybe** I will visit Paris.
	You are **too** young.
time:	
today, now, on Sunday etc.	
We have a test **today**.	

Note: locução adverbial (adverbial phrase) – conjunto de palavras que exercem a função de advérbio: in silence, under the sea, in an hour, by the ocean etc.

Exercises [answers on p. 181]

1 Classify the underlined adverbs as M (manner), P (place), T (time), F (frequecy) and D (doubt/degree).

1. That house is <u>quite</u> expensive.   _D_
2. She speaks <u>slowly</u>.   _____
3. He ran <u>fast</u> to catch the bus.   _____
4. He wants to go <u>downstairs</u>.   _____

A | 19

5. He is rarely capable of doing the task. _____
6. We study French daily. _____
7. He seldom sleeps late. _____
8. Let's leave now. _____
9. I could hardly breathe. _____
10. We are probably late. _____
11. Maybe we can meet you after the test. _____
12. The kids are playing upstairs. _____

2 Choose the correct words to complete the sentences.

1. She _____ *really* _____ loves cooking.
   a. much   b. good   c. really ✓
2. If you arrive late, come in _____ please.
   a. silently   b. there   c. now
3. Leave your things _____ and come down for a cup of tea.
   a. under the sea b. upstairs   c. easily
4. I can't understand him. He doesn't speak very _____ .
   a. slowly   b. clearly   c. seldom
5. He played the flute beautifully _____ .
   a. yesterday   b. badly   c. well
6. Did you see George _____ ?
   a. tomorrow   b. fluently   c. last week
7. Do they _____ behave like that?
   a. monthly   b. very   c. always
8. They didn't want to get up. _____ it was too _____ .
   a. Gently – late b. Perhaps – very c. Maybe – early
9. Why do you walk _____ slowly?
   a. so   b. enough   c. nearly
10. We spent the day _____ .
    a. by the ocean b. in the afternoon c. perhaps

7 Adverbs II

Form & spelling

Alguns **advérbios** têm forma própria: **fast, here, now, often, perhaps** etc. Outros têm formação irregular: good → **well**

Muitos são formados acrescentando-se **-ly** a diversos tipos de palavras:

sad – sad**ly**   easy – easi**ly**   real – real**ly**

Spelling

A maioria das palavras não sofre alteração ao receber **-ly** mas palavras terminadas em...

1. -y mudam y para i: laz**y** – laz**ily** heav**y** – heav**ily** angr**y** – angr**ily**	**3. -l** dobram o -l: rea**l** – rea**lly** loya**l** – loya**lly** annua**l** – annua**lly**
2. -ic recebem -ally: econom**ic** – econom**ically** trag**ic** – trag**ically** dynam**ic** – dynam**ically**	**4. -able/-ible, -le, -e** perdem o -e: comfort**able** – comfort**ably** poss**ible** – poss**ibly** tru**e** – tru**ly**

Note – nem todas as palavras perdem o -e final ao receber -ly: rarely, purely, etc.

Exercises [answers on p. 182]

1 Transform the adjectives below into adverbs.

1. gentle — *gently*
2. simple — _____
3. loud — _____

4. happy _____
5. basic _____
6. angry _____
7. terrible _____
8. boring _____
9. careful _____
10. probable _____

2 **Complete the sentences using adverbs.**

1. The dog ran _____*quickly*_____ . (quick)
2. She is always _____ dressed. (beautiful)
3. The results were _____ good. (relative)
4. Ann spoke about Grandpa _____ . (nice)
5. Joe spoke about his job _____ . (dramatic)
6. The teacher solved the problem _____ . (easy)
7. The children laughed _____ . (happy)
8. They are writing too _____ . (slow)
9. The people were _____ dressed. (poor)
10. My father drives very _____ . (careful)

3 **Check the correct words to complete the sentences.**

1. The crime occurred _____*shortly*_____ before 3 a.m.
   a. short   b. shortly ✓
2. John Lennon was a _____ great musician.
   a. truly   b. truely
3. It is _____ difficult to explain things to people.
   a. extremely   b. extremly
4. We don't _____ understand what he says.
   a. fully   b. full
5. My neighbor drives _____ .
   a. carelessly   b. carelly
6. You can _____ see famous actors in this district.
   a. frequent   b. frequently
7. Governments have to _____ care about the environment.
   a. seriously   b. serious
8. This is _____ the best restaurant in London.
   a. easily   b. easyly

8 Adverbs III

Position

A posição mais comum para advérbios e locuções adverbiais é no final da frase. Dependendo do tipo, podem também ser colocados no início da frase ou, depois de verbo auxiliar ou ainda antes do verbo principal.

1. início (ênfase)	2. final
a maioria dos advérbios:	manner, place, time:
Slowly he walked home.	He drives **slowly**.
Here they go.	He went **there**.
Yesterday they got up late.	He arrived **yesterday**.

3. após verbo auxiliar/antes do verbo principal
degree, doubt, frequency:
He is **very** late.
I can **probably** meet him.
He **usually** drives slowly.

Note – vários advérbios juntos geralmente vêm na ordem: manner / place / time.
Ex: She cried sadly **at home yesterday**.

Exercises [answers on p. 182]

1 Underline the correct answer.

1. He drove the bus (<u>carefully</u> – probably).
2. She speaks English (well – very).
3. I (up – rarely) walk the dog.
4. I didn't see them (quickly – there).
5. We treated the students (respectfully – already).
6. You should talk to him (enough – as soon as possible).
7. (Quite – Tomorrow) he will tell us the truth.
8. We go fishing (in summer – perhaps).
9. I (extremely – seldom) have fish for lunch.
10. She is (much – usually) here in January.

2 Rewrite the words given in the correct place.

1. How does he drive?
   (fast) He _____ drives _____*fast*_____ .
2. Where did you go yesterday?
   (to the club) We _____ went _____ yesterday.
3. When did you arrive here?
   (in December) I _____ arrived here _____ .
4. When are you going to Japan?
   (next year) I _____ am going to Japan _____ .
5. Can you open this can?
   (easily) Yes, I _____ can _____ open that can.
6. Is Mike handsome?
   (really) Yes, he _____ is _____ handsome.
7. How did they behave at school?
   (badly) _____ they _____ behaved.
8. Why didn't they go to the show?
   (Unfortunately) _____ they missed the _____ bus.
9. When are you leaving?
   (now) We _____ are leaving right _____ .
10. Did she talk to you when she left?
    (silently) No, she _____ left _____ .

9 Adverbs IV

Order

Para evitar problemas de compreensão é preciso observar a ordem em que os advérbios em série devem ser usados.

1. dois advérbios	2. expressões do mesmo tipo
manner, time: I work **hard every day**. place, time: I arrived **there late**. place, manner: He left **school quickly**.	a mais específica vem antes: I was born **at 5 p.m.**, January, 2001.

3. três ou mais advérbios

subj. / v.	manner	place	frequency	time
I sing	happily	in my room	every day	in the morning.
He runs	quickly	around the lake	usually	after dinner.
She walks	slowly	into town	weekly	before lunch.

Exercises [answers on p. 183]

1 Rewrite the sentences and place the words given in the correct place.

1. We arrived (last week, in Jamaica).
   We arrived in Jamaica last week.
2. It is (this morning, very windy).

3. You studied (yesterday, very hard).

4. He went (in a hurry, there).

5. She closed the door (carefully, very).

6. She finished the last chapter (yesterday, very quickly, at home).

7. I studied (in the library, peacefully, yesterday).

2 Check the wrong sentences.

1. She walked slowly into the room before dinner. _____
2. Sometimes she drives to work in the morning. _____
3. We have recently visited him. _____
4. They work hard at home twice a week. _____
5. He joined quickly his group for dinner. _____
6. I easily could find the way to the park. _____
7. He was born in 2010, in December's. _____
8. They wanted to buy a new car very badly. _____
9. We really enjoyed the trip to South Port. _____
10. I have lived in Nebraska, in a brick house. _____

10 Adverb or Adjective?

Advérbios modificam verbos, adjetivos, outros advérbios ou frases inteiras. **Adjetivos** modificam substantivos ou pronomes.

adverb	adjective

He drives **fast**.
    (verbo)
She is **really** nice.
    (adj.)
He dances **very** well.
    (adv.)
Fortunately she was not home.
    (frase)
	My friend has a **fast** car.
	                    (subst.)
	The **old** man is here.
	    (subst.)
	She is **happy**.
	(pron.)

Certas palavras funcionam tanto como advérbio quanto como adjetivo:

close   deep   early   fast   hard   high   late   long   low   wide   etc.

adverb	adjective
She came **close** and talked to me. She works **hard**.	He is a **close** friend of mine. It's **hard** work.

Exercises [answers on p. 183]

1 Circle the adverbs and underline the adjectives.
1. The grizzly bear is a large predator.
2. He ran fast to catch the bus.
3. I will always remember them.
4. I get up early.
5. I caught the early bus.
6. The birth of gunpowder was accidental.
7. The cheetah runs incredibly quickly.

A | 27

8. The general atmosphere at the meeting was great.
9. He lives exceedingly far.
10. The students' feedback was extremely positive.

2 Complete the sentences with words from the box. Use each word twice.

> ~~early~~   late   deep   long   low

1. They left unusually _____ *early* _____.
2. Take a _____ breath and calm down.
3. We worked _____ into the night.
4. John arrived _____.
5. That plane is flying _____.
6. He sat down and told us a _____ story.
7. The teacher put the books is a _____ shelf.
8. I'm watching the _____ film.
9. How _____ did they stay?
10. _____ explorers used the stars for navigation.

3 Choose the correct form to complete the sentences.
1. She is (extreme, extremely) _____ *extremely* _____ confident.
2. He speaks (soft, softly) _____.
3. This is a (hard, hardly) _____ problem.
4. He walked to the park (slow, slowly) _____.
5. The birds were flying (surprising, surprisingly) _____ low.
6. Liverpool is a lively, (modern, modernly) _____ city.
7. She knows the Italian culture very (good, well) _____.
8. Why does she dress so (poor, poorly) _____?
9. She did a (fantastic, fantastically) _____ job with that song.
10. The impala is a (small, smally) _____ African antelope.

28 | A

11 Adverb List

Manner, place, time

Manner
Geralmente terminados em **-ly**.

angrily	gladly	madly	shyly
badly	happily	nervously	**so**
busily	**hard**	openly	**straight**
calmly	honestly	patiently	tenderly
carefully	hungrily	politely	unexpectedly
easily	irritably	quickly	violently
exactly	justly	rapidly	warmly
fast*	kindly	roughly	**well**
frankly	lazily	rudely	wildly
gently	loudly	sadly	etc.

Note: As palavras em negrito funcionam como advérbios ou adjetivos.

Place
Alguns advérbios de lugar funcionam também como preposição:

She put the scarf **on** the table.

about	below	in	outside
above	down	indoors	over
abroad	downstairs	inside	there
anywhere	east (etc.)	near	towards
away	elsewhere	nearby	under
back	everywhere	off	up
backward/s	far	on	upstairs
behind	here	out	where

Ver Prepositions, p. 137.

Time

already	**first**	lately	recently	today
before	formerly	later	since	tomorrow
earlier	**just**	**next**	soon	tonight
early*	**last**	now	**still**	yesterday
finally	**late**	previously	then	yet

Frequency

annually	nightly	constantly	never	regularly
daily	quarterly	ever	normally	seldom
fortnightly	**weekly**	frequently	occasionally	sometimes
hourly	**yearly**	generally	often	regularly
monthly	always	infrequently	rarely	usually

Degree

almost	extremely	intensely	positively	somewhat
absolutely	fairly	**just**	practically	strongly
badly*	**far**	least	**pretty**	terribly
barely	fully	less	purely	thoroughly
completely	greatly	**little**	quite	too
decidedly	hardly	lots	rather	totally
deeply	highly	most	really	utterly
enough	how	much	scarcely	very
enormously	incredibly	nearly	simply	virtually
entirely	indeed	perfectly	so	well

Note: As palavras em negrito funcionam como advérbios ou adjetivos.

12 Agreement

Subject & verb

1. Usa-se verbo no singular com

sujeito no singular e quantias:
That girl **loves** you.
Five years **is** a long time.

coletivos*, nomes de organizações, países:
The family **was** at the table.
GM **has** announced its new line.
The USA **is** a big country.

palavras de significado singular como blues, ethics, politics, news etc.:
The news **is** bad.

indefinidos terminados em -one, -body, -thing:
Everyone **wants** to leave early.
Nothing **makes** me cry.

(n)either, each, other, another, one (of), less, little, much etc.:
Either dress **suits** me.
Each of them **is** fine.

2. Usa-se verbo no singular ou no plural com

all, any, some e none:
Some of the money **is** missing.
Some of the students **are** hungry.

3. Usa-se verbo no plural com

sujeito no plural:
The students **were** at the gym.
Mistakes **are** not a problem here.

palavras de significado plural como scissors, pants, glasses etc:
My pants **are** torn.
My scissors **were** lost.

os coletivos police e people, nomes de times esportivos:
The police **have** arrested him.
The Yankees **have** signed a new third baseman.

both, few, many, several, (the) others, several:
Several **were** dismissed.

* exceto **police** e **people**

Exercises [answers on p. 184]

1 Underline the correct verb form.

1. Any drink (<u>is</u>, are) fine for me.
2. Where are they? All (is, are) lost.
3. Both (is, are) my friends.
4. Everything left (is, are) going to be sold.
5. One sang while the other (was, were) playing the piano.
6. Thirty thousand dollars (is, are) a lot of money.
7. None of the girls (is, are) related to me.

8. None of the pie (is, are) left.
9. Police (is, are) investigating the incident.
10. One of the reasons we do this (is, are) that it rains a lot in spring.

2 Underline the correct verb form.

1. Nobody (<u>thinks</u>, think) you are mean.
2. Few (is, **are**) going to believe you.
3. One of the students in this room (is, are) responsible.
4. The government (is, are) doing a good job.
5. Chelsea Brothers (is, are) the best company in town.
6. Many (agrees, agree) with you.
7. Mathematics (is, are) said to be difficult.
8. Many sons (dislikes, dislike) their father.
9. You (feels, feel) like a fish out of water.
10. Five years (is, are) a long time.

3 Underline the correct verb form.

1. They say we (is, <u>are</u>) too young.
2. Others (has, have) said the same thing.
3. Anyone (is, are) going to see this.
4. Juice or tea? Either (is, are) fine.
5. People (is, are) usually happy at home.
6. My favorite breakfast (is, are) cereal with fruit and milk.
7. Less time (is, are) spent with the family.
8. Each student (has, have) his seat.
9. Ten miles (is, are) a long way to walk.
10. Much (was, were) discussed at the meeting.

13 Articles

Indefinite & definite

Artigos vêm junto a substantivos. Indicam se o substantivo se refere a algo genérico (artigo indefinido) ou a algo específico (artigo definido).

um livro	**uma** bola	**o** livro	**a** bola
(a book)	(a ball)	(the book)	(the ball)

1. indefinite article
a/n (um, uma) **é usado com:**

a – sons consonantais:
a girl   **a** hippo
a uniform   **a** university

an – sons vocálicos:
an egg   **an** ugly cup
an hour   **an** honest girl

2. definite article
the (o/s, a/s) **é usado com:**

substantivos em geral (precedidos ou não por adjetivos):
the boy   **the** sad girl
the bank   **the** piano

superlativos, adjetivos usados como substantivos:
the best man **the** oldest book
the poor   **the** rich

nomes de países (plural), grupos de ilhas ou montanhas:
the Philippines   **the** Alps
the United States

nomes de pontos cardeais, mares, rios, desertos:
the south of Cuba **the** Atlantic
the Volga River   **the** Sahara

nomes de famílias, bandas, nacionalidades, títulos de livros, filmes, hotéis, jornais, navios, edifícios, organizações:
the Garcias   **the** Doors
the French   **the** Ritz
the CNN   **the** Titanic
The Lord of the Rings

Note – Por modificarem substantivos, artigos funcionam como adjetivos.

Exercises [answers on p. 184]

1 Fill in the blanks with the correct indefinite article.

1. _an_ eye
2. _____ ear
3. _____ hospital
4. _____ house
5. _____ honest person
6. _____ rich girl
7. _____ animal
8. _____ room
9. _____ hot day
10. _____ uniform

2 Fill in the blanks with the definite article, if needed.

1. He went to _____ British Islands on vacation.
2. Maria looked out _____ window.
3. We spend a week at _____ Hilton annually.
4. _____ employees are paid monthly.
5. _____ chair is badly made.
6. Jean plays _____ piano well.
7. _____ people were disappointed by the election results.
8. It was an honor to be invited to _____ ceremony.
9. He studied the sun, the moon and the movement of _____ stars.
10. South America is bordered on the west by _____ Pacific Ocean.

3 Underline the correct answer.

1. Agatha Christie was born in (the, —) England in 1890.
2. She was (a, an) English crime novelist and (a, an) short story writer.
3. She published her first novel in 1920 and became one of (the, a) most famous writers in history.
4. She wrote mystery stories like Murder at (a, the) Vicarage.
5. Many of her stories revolve around (an, the) investigations of characters such as Hercule Poirot, Miss Jane and Tommy and Tuppence.
6. She wrote (a, the) world's longest running play, (The, —) Mousetrap.
7. The Mousetrap is (a, an) murder mystery play. It opened in (—, the) West End of London in 1952 and has been running since then.
8. Sir Arthur Ignatius Conan Doyle (1859-1930) was (a, an) Scottish physician and writer.
9. He wrote fictional stories about (a, the) detective Sherlock Holmes.
10. Doyle was employed as (a, an) ship surgeon on (the, —) SS Mayumba during (a, an) voyage to (the, —) West African coast, in 1880.

14 Auxiliary & Modal Verbs

Em inglês o verbo principal da frase é chamado verbo **comum** ou principal (main/ common/ ordinary verb). Pode aparecer sozinho ou acompanhado por um **verbo auxiliar**.

I **work**.   I am **working**.   I can **work**.   Does he **work**?

Se um verbo precede o verbo principal, é considerado um verbo auxiliar. Alguns dos auxiliares são chamados simplesmente de **auxiliares** (auxiliary verbs), outros são chamados de **modais** (modal verbs).

De modo geral qualquer auxiliar:

→ faz negativas: I am **not**   We can**not**
→ faz interrogativas: **Am** I?   **Can** we?
→ tem formas contraídas: **I'm**   We **can't**

Auxiliary Verbs	Modal Verbs
Be, do e *have* são auxiliares; auxiliam o verbo principal em formas e tempos verbais: I **am** cooking. **Do** you swim? He **has** arrived. *Be, do* e *have* podem funcionar como verbos auxiliares ou como verbos comuns: I **am** a cook. I **do** my job. He **has** a dog. [ver Be, Do, Have p. 39, 61, 77]	Auxiliam o verbo principal a expressar conceitos como possibilidade, conselho etc.: You **should** see a doctor. *Can, could, may, might, will, would, must, shall, should,* e *ought* to são auxiliares modais. I **can** swim. He **could** help. I **must** move. It **may** rain. He **shall** leave. I **should** go. [ver Modal Auxiliaries p. 95]

Exercises [answers on p. 185]

1. Classify the underlined words as A (for auxiliary verb) or O (for ordinary verb).

1. Where <u>does</u> your brother work? _A_
2. They <u>have</u> decided to advertise their house. ____
3. He <u>does</u> his homework on the way to school. ____
4. The story <u>was</u> truly funny. ____
5. I will <u>have</u> the soup. ____
6. John <u>is</u> seriously ill. ____
7. He <u>was</u> driving carelessly. ____
8. We<u>'re</u> going out at 7:00 tonight. ____
9. Do you <u>have</u> a headache? ____
10. Policemen are <u>investigating</u> the incident. ____

2. Classify the underlined words as M (for modal verb) or O (for ordinary verb).

1. They should <u>have</u> time for a quick meal. _O_
2. She <u>speaks</u> six languages. ____
3. Who shall <u>drive</u> the car? ____
4. John <u>can</u> speak French fluently. ____
5. What <u>could</u> we do? ____
6. The class president <u>called</u> off the meeting. ____
7. He was so tired that he <u>could</u> hardly speak. ____
8. When will you <u>stop</u> smoking? ____
9. <u>May</u> I have some more water? ____
10. You should <u>check</u> the schedule out. ____

3. Underline the correct alternative.

1. There are things you can't (do, be) when traveling by plane. You can't (make, take) any objects in your hand baggage that could (cause, help) injury to yourself and other passengers.
2. You can't (carry, observe) more than one lighter and you should (drive, put) it inside a plastic bag.
3. You must (call, keep) the lighter on your person throughout the flight.

15 Basic Sentence Patterns

Em inglês toda sentença tem como base **sujeito e verbo**. Outros componentes – **objetos e complementos** – quando acrescentados a esses dois elementos, formam padrões básicos de sentenças.

I read.   I am a teacher.   I read books.   I read books to the children.

1. S-V[1]			**3. S-V-O**		
subject + verb			subject + verb + object/s		
He	sings	every day.[2]	He	likes	books.
He	is	there.)	He	gave	it to me.
He	sleeps	on the sofa.	He	gave	me a book.
(S)	(V)		(S)	(V)	(O)
2. S-V-C			**4. (S-V-O-C)**			
subject + linking verb[3] + complement			subject + verb + object + complement			
I	am	his mother.	I	left	the door	open.
He	looks	sad.	I	named	him	'Cat'.
(S)	(LV)	(C)	(S)	(V)	(O)	(C)

Notes – **(1)** abbreviations: **S** = subject; **V** = verb; **LV** = linking verb; **O** = object; **C** = complement; **(2)** desconsidere advérbios para analisar as estruturas; **(3) Linking Verbs** fornecem informações adicionais sobre o sujeito: be, become, feel, seem etc.

Os padrões básicos podem ser expandidos para formar frases mais complexas.

Exercises [answers on p. 185]

1 Circle SV or SVO to classify the sentence pattern.

1. The dogs are sleeping in the garage.   (SV)   SVO
2. Those guards gave him a book.   SV   SVO
3. Joe plays the guitar.   SV   SVO
4. They borrowed some money.   SV   SVO

5.	Erika paid him a low salary.	SV	SVO
6.	She sleeps on the sofa.	SV	SVO
7.	Spring rain and flowers abound.	SV	SVO
8.	She teaches English to us.	SV	SVO
9.	That garbage man surfs.	SV	SVO
10.	Those boys told her the direction.	SV	SVO

2 Circle SVC or SVOC to classify the sentence pattern.

1.	I called him 'the detective'.	SVC	(SVOC)
2.	I heard the girl crying.	SVC	SVOC
3.	Your sister seems angry.	SVC	SVOC
4.	My brother became a doctor.	SVC	SVOC
5.	Mr. Watson is the teacher.	SVC	SVOC
6.	They named her Alice.	SVC	SVOC
7.	The workers are lazy.	SVC	SVOC
8.	We elected him president.	SVC	SVOC
9.	He is fine.	SVC	SVOC
10.	That man got the TV repaired.	SVC	SVOC

3 Complete the sentences with the correct complement from the box.

> comfortable   ~~doctors~~   drive   fixed   French
> intelligent   mad   mom   open   Woolly

1. The men are _____ *doctors* _____
2. They had him _____
3. She is my _____
4. I left the door _____
5. The girl thinks herself _____
6. Our house is _____
7. Cats drove the dogs _____
8. The children called it "_____"
9. Those workers got their watches _____
10. That woman teaches us _____

16 Be

Present & past

O verbo **to be** (ser; estar) pode ser usado como verbo principal ou como verbo auxiliar. Quando auxiliar, ajuda um verbo principal a formar tempos contínuos e voz passiva.

He **is** tired.
(principal)

He **was** *sleeping*.
(auxiliar)

The houses **were** *sold* by me.
(auxiliar)

Present (affirmative)		Past (affirmative)	
I **am**	We **are**	I **was**	We **were**
You **are**	You **are**	You **were**	You **were**
He, she it **is**	They **are**	He, she, it **was**	They **were**

Forms	
interrogative: **Is** he tired? **Was** he working? negative: He is **not** tired. He was **not** working. negative-interrogative: **Isn't** he tired? **Wasn't** he working?	question: **Who** is he? **What** was he singing? short answer: Yes, he **is**. No, he **isn't**. contracted form: are: **'re** am: **'m** is: **'s** am not: **'m not** is not: **isn't** are not: **aren't** was not: **wasn't** were not: **weren't**

Notes – **interrogative:** auxiliar antes do sujeito; **question:** palavra interrogativa antes do auxiliar; **negative:** auxiliar + not; **negative-interrogative:** auxiliar negativo e contraído antes do sujeito.

Exercises [answers on p. 186]

1 Complete the sentences with the correct form of to be.

1. The Republic of India _____is_____ a country in Asia.
2. The capital _____ New Delhi.
3. Two classical languages, Sanskrit and Tamil _____ born in India.
4. Today, Hindi and English _____ the official languages.
5. Mahatma Gandhi _____ a famous leader in India in 1947.
6. He _____ a non-violent activist in the movement for the independence of the country.
7. Pakistan, Bangladesh, China, Myanmar, Bhutan, and Nepal _____ countries next to India.
8. The beautiful Taj Mahal, in the city of Agra, _____ built in the 17th century.
9. Over 10,000 people _____ used to build it.
10. The Lotus flower and the Bengal tiger _____ national symbols.

2 Turn the sentences into the negative form.

1. He was a very intelligent man.   *He was not (wasn't) a very intelligent man.*
2. They were late for the show.   _____
3. The musician is busy today.   _____
4. Muse is the name of a band.   _____
5. I am a good rock singer.   _____

3 Turn the sentences into the interrogative form.

1. Lollapalooza is an annual music festival.
   Is Lollapalooza an annual music festival?
2. Tony Bennet and Frank Sinatra were famous singers.
   _____
3. The national bird of Brazil is the Sabiá-laranjeira.
   _____
4. Jaguars and sea turtles are endangered species.
   _____
5. Castro Alves was a famous poet.
   _____

17 Collective & Compound Nouns

Substantivos coletivos (Collective Nouns) nomeiam conjuntos de itens ou de seres de uma mesma espécie. Podem aparecer no plural, mas são geralmente usados no singular e a concordância é feita com o singular.

A **flock** of tourists **has** arrived.   **Flocks** of birds **are flying** south.

item: collective
- bees: **swarm**
- firefighters: **brigade**
- fish: **school**
- flowers: **bouquet**
- friends: **party**
- elephant: **herd**
- islands: **archipelago**
- lions: **pride**
- mountains: **range**
- people: **crowd**
- puppies: **litter**
- sailors: **crew**
- sheep, geese, tourists, etc.: **flock**
- thieves: **gang**
- wolves: **pack**

Substantivos compostos (Compound Nouns) são formados pela junção de diferentes classes de palavras como substantivos, adjetivos, verbos etc.

I need a **haircut**.   Where is the **bus stop**?   He is my **father-in-law**.

noun + noun:	**tennis** shoe **foot**ball	adj. + verb:	**good**will **dead**lock
noun + verb:	**sun**rise **hair**cut	verb + noun:	break**fast** flying **machine**
noun + adjective:	**truck**ful **mouth**ful	prep. + noun:	under**ground** out**law**
adj + noun:	full **moon** green**house**	adv. + noun:	by**stander** over**coat**
		others:	check-in standstill

Note – Se a 1ª palavra termina originalmente em **-s** *(clothes, sports etc.)*, mantêm-se o **-s**: *clothes shops, sports store.*

Exercises [answers on p. 186]

1 Complete the sentences with collectives from the box.

> archipelago   bouquet   litter   ~~crew~~   pride   pack   herd   class   pride

1. The captain arrived with ten members of his _____crew_____.
2. We went to the Zoo to see the _____ of lions that had arrived from Africa.
3. He said that the wolves were hungry. The _____ attacked the camping site and stole their food.
4. I would like to know the Canary Islands _____ located in the Atlantic Ocean.
5. We followed the elephants all night long. Finally, in the morning, we could approach the _____.
6. Bingo gave birth to ten puppies. It was a healthy _____.
7. The _____ of cattle was slowly crossing the river.
8. He gave her a _____ of red roses.
9. The _____ of lions was relaxing in the sun.

2 Check the words that form compound nouns.

1.	tooth	a. paste ✓	b. hit	c. home
2.	hair-	a. brushing	b. going	c. moving
3.	court-	a. ball	b. army	c. martial
4.	black	a. blue	b. board	c. book
5.	safe	a. doing	b. keeping	c. helping
6.	swimming	a. room	b. door	c. pool
7.	sub	a. way	b. road	c. street
8.	out	a. in	b. put	c. take
9.	race	a. fly	b. zebra	c. horse

3 Form new words from the words below.

1. race: _horse race, boat race_
2. station: _____
3. tennis: _____
4. moon: _____
5. clothes: _____

42 | C

18 Conditional Sentences (if clauses)

Use

Orações condicionais (if clauses) expressam alguns tipos de condição ou hipótese e vêm sempre ligadas a uma oração principal (main clause).

If you drink that, **you will feel sick**.
(if clause)   (main clause)

Por meio dessas construções é possível expressar:

1. zero conditional ordens, leis naturais. If you go to LA, **visit San Diego**. If you heat water, **it evaporates**.	**3. 2nd conditional** situações pouco prováveis. If I had money, **I would buy a car**.
2. 1st conditional situações possíveis. If I buy a bike, **I will ride to work**.	**4. 3rd conditional** situações impossíveis. If he had gone, **I would have saved him**.

Na oração principal, além dos tempos Presente, Futuro e Imperativo usa-se também:

Simple Conditional (would + verbo): I would go.	**Conditional Perfect** (would have + verbo pp[1]): I would[2] have gone.

Notes – (1) pp = particípio passado; **(2) formas abreviadas –** would: 'd, would not: wouldn't.

Exercises [answers on p. 187]

1 Rewrite the sentences. Use the Simple Conditional.
1. I will go to the club next week.   *I would go to the club next week.*
2. Will you work next Monday?
3. He will not (won't) come today.
4. The teachers will help us.
5. You won't meet him.

2 Rewrite the sentences. Use the Conditional Perfect.
1. She would live in Japan.   *She would have lived in Japan.*
2. They would sell the car.
3. I wouldn't leave home.
4. Would you buy a bike?
5. Would they teach us?

3 Circle the correct meaning: P (possible), U (unlikely) or (I) impossible.
1. If I knew his address, I would visit him.   P (U) I
2. If I had known that you were ill, I would have visited you.   P U I
3. You will be ill if you eat all that.   P U I
4. If I see her, I'll kiss her.   P U I
5. If he had asked me, I'd have accepted it.   P U I
6. If I won the prize, I'd give up my job.   P U I
7. If he reads in the dark, he'll ruin his eyes.   P U I
8. If they cooked dinner, I'd be very happy.   P U I
9. She would have baked a cake if we had asked her.   P U I
10. If he had a degree, he would get a job easily.   P U I

4 Check the correct alternative.
1. If you go to the movies, I will (go, gone) too.
2. If they were here, they would (talk, talked) to him.
3. If he had left early, he wouldn't have (miss, missed) the bus.
4. We won't (see, seen) them if we arrive late.
5. He would (be, been) angry if you took his picture.
6. I would have (stopped, stop) if I had seen the old man.

19 Conditional Sentences II

Verb tenses

A sequência de verbos a ser usada com **orações condicionais** depende do que se deseja expressar.

condition	If clause	main clause
(zero) general truth: order:	simple present If[1] you **heat** ice, If you **love** him,	simple present/ imperative it **turns** to water. **talk** to him.
(1st) possible:	simple present If he **sings** that song,	will + verbo we will **leave** the room.
(2nd) unlikely:	simple past If he **were**[2] tired,	would + verbo he **wouldn't talk** so much.
(3rd) impossible:	past perfect If you **had asked** us,	would have + verbo pp[3] we **would have done** it.

Notes – (1) unless (= if not: a menos que, se não): I'll be back today **unless** there is a bus strike; **(2) to be** (2nd conditional): usa-se **were** para todas as pessoas: If I **were** you, I would call him; **(3) pp**: particípio passado.

Exercises [answers on p. 188]

1 Complete the sentences. Use the verbs given.

1. If ice gets hot, it _____ *melts* _____ (melt).
2. He _____ (accept) the job unless the salary is too low.
3. I _____ (do) it if I have enough time.
4. If you can't walk, _____ (take) a taxi.
5. He _____ (come) if we call him.
6. If you don't pay attention, you _____ (break) it.
7. If it rains, we _____ (get) wet.
8. _____ you _____ (help) me if I need you?

C | 45

2 Complete the sentences. Use the verbs given.

1. They _____would come_____ (come) if you called them.
2. I _____ (be) pleased if you came.
3. He _____ (reach) it if he were tall enough.
4. If I could, I _____ (answer) it.
5. If I were you, I _____ (go) home now.
6. If it rained, we _____ (stay) home.
7. If you went away, they _____ (be) very sad.
8. _____ you _____ (help) me if I needed you?

3 Complete the sentences. Use the verbs given.

1. I _____would have done_____ (do) it if I had known how to.
2. He _____ (come) if you had called him.
3. If he had known that, he _____ (make – neg.) a mistake.
4. If you had waited, I _____ (be) happy.
5. He _____ (tell) you if you had asked him.
6. If you had jumped over it, you _____ (break) your leg.
7. If they had thought better, they _____ (go – neg.) there.
8. _____ you _____ (help) me if I had needed you?

4 Check the correct alternative.

1. He _____will come_____ if you wait.
   a. will come ✓   b. would come   c. would have come
2. If you rang the bell, I _____ .
   a. will come   b. would come   c. would have come
3. If he had written to me, I _____ to him.
   a. write   b. would write   c. would have written
4. If you had opened the door, you _____ us.
   a. will see   b. would have seen   c. would see
5. If they saw us, they _____ to us.
   a. would speak   b. will speak   c. would have spoken
6. What _____ you _____ if you meet him?
   a. will – do   b. would – do   c. would – have done
7. _____ you _____ him if you saw him?
   a. Will – invite   b. Would – have invited   c. Would – invite
8. _____ you _____ the car if you had won the money?
   a. Will – buy   b. Would – buy   c. Would – have bought

20 Conjunctions I

Conjunções são palavras como *and, or, but, however* etc. São usadas para juntar palavras, frases ou partes de orações.

1. as mais comuns são:

and (e):
I fell down **and** broke my left foot.

but (mas):
I bought a small **but** good car.

for (pois, porque):
I was angry, **for** I didn't speak Italian.

nor (nem):
He won't wait for you **nor** for me.

or (ou):
Bring me some tea **or** coffee, please.

so (assim, portanto):
Call me later, **so** we can talk about it.

yet (contudo):
He can't act well, **yet** he can sing beautifully.

2. algumas são usadas em pares:

as well as (assim como):
Joe, **as well as** Sue, is a Math teacher.

both ... and (ambos ... e):
Both he **and** his sister are good actors.

either...or (ou...ou):
Either go now **or** after dinner.

neither ... nor (nem ... nem):
Neither he **nor** she wants to travel by plane.

not only ... but also
(não só ... mas também):
She **not only** sings, **but also** dances well.

whether ... or (quer ... quer, se ... ou):
I'll go to the party **whether** she comes **or** not.

Exercises [answers on p. 188]

1 Underline the correct alternative.

1. Do you want the red apple (<u>or</u>, but) the green one?
2. The kids arrived home (so, and) went straight to bed.
3. I am going to the Zoo with Kyle (and, for) Pete.
4. We couldn't stay, (and, for) it was too cold.
5. I like that song very much, (but, so) I downloaded it.
6. You can have (neither, either) apples or pears.

7. He is handsome (but, for) he is very rude.
8. She speaks not only English (both, but also) French very well.

2 **Complete the sentences with words from the box.**

also both both ~~for~~ neither so so yet

1. I want to go there again, _____*for*_____ it is a wonderful place.
2. Not only red but _____ blue looks good on you.
3. I am _____ happy and excited.
4. I got _____ the card nor the envelope.
5. The day was cold, _____ sunny.
6. We went home early, _____ we missed the end of the play.
7. These exercises are _____ easy and useful.
8. He didn't show up, _____ we left without him.

3 **Check the wrong sentences and correct the mistakes.**

1. Those people are rich but also they aren't happy.
   _____

2. My friend neither called nor wrote.
   _____

3. He is either a fool or a genius.
   _____

4. The dogs, as well as the cats, are sleeping.
   _____

5. Both Jane but Ann are correct.
   _____

6. We were not late, and we walked slowly.
   _____

7. You must do it whether you want to or not.
   _____

8. He writes well, yet I don't like his articles.
   _____

21 Conjunctions II

3. observe mais alguns exemplos:

after (depois que):
I can show you the letter **after** I have read it.

although (embora):
Although I arrived early I couldn't talk to him.

as (da mesma forma; enquanto; como):
Do **as** I do./ **As** I left the room I remembered the bag.

as if, as though (como se):
They treated us **as if** we were strangers.

as soon as (assim que):
As soon as I finish, I'll let you know.

because (porque, devido a):
She won't follow us **because** she is tired.

before (antes que):
Come back **before** it gets dark.

even if (mesmo que, ainda que):
I won't talk to him **even if** you ask me to.

however (contudo):
She betrayed our secret, **however**, I forgive her.

if (se):
If you want to go now, I'll go with you.

like (como):
To act **like** he does, requires great memory.

once (quando; uma vez que):
Once they go, we can take a nap./ **Once** you find a new job, you can marry her.

provided that (desde que):
We'll come **provided that** we are invited.

since (desde que, visto que):
You can stay here **since** you keep calm.

therefore (portanto):
I don't like him, **therefore** I decided not to call him.

though (embora):
He went out with her **though** he didn't want to.

unless (a menos que):
You won't succeed **unless** you study hard.

until (até que):
Wait **until** I come back.

when (quando):
When it rains, the taxis disappear.

whenever (quando quer que):
I smile **whenever** I remember that day.

where (onde):
Grandma lives **where** the climate is mild.

wherever (onde quer que):
He makes friends **wherever** he goes.

whether (se):
I wonder **whether** he will do what he said.

while (enquanto que; enquanto):
I am punctual, **while** you are always late./ It was lovely **while** it lasted.

Exercises [answers on p. 189]

1 **Underline the correct alternative.**

1. She was late, (<u>however</u>, because) she was not punished.
2. He was lazy, (therefore, unless) he failed.
3. Stay inside (where, while) it's raining.
4. I didn't go to work (because, until) I was ill.
5. (Once, Before) you are finished, you can leave.
6. Come (whenever, even if) you like.
7. (Whether, As) it grew darker it became colder.
8. He laughed (unless, until) the teacher called him.

2 **Check the correct sentences.**

1. They went home because the children wanted to.   ✓
2. They went home before the concert ended.   ____
3. They went home because they were tired.   ____
4. They went home after the Muse had finished the show.   ____
5. They went home although they wanted to stay longer.   ____

22 Countable & Uncountable Nouns

Em Inglês, os substantivos podem ser **contáveis** (countable) ou **incontáveis** (uncountable).

Countable nouns[1]	**Uncountable nouns**[2]
referem-se a itens que podem ser contados individualmente – pessoas, coisas, animais: a **boy**, two **chairs**, three **cats**. são usados no singular ou no plural: The **chair** is expensive. The **girls** are hungry. My **dog** loves cats.	referem-se a itens que não podem ser contados de forma individual – substâncias, ideias, atividades e qualidades: water, oxygen, gold, freedom, love, acting, work, courage. são usados no singular. This news **is** important. This coffee **is** delicious.

É possível mensurar itens incontáveis acrescentando-se a eles palavras como: **bar – bottle – box – kilo – liter – loaf – slice – piece** etc.
Buy two **loaves** of bread, please.
I want two **bars** of chocolate.

Notes – (1) **São incontáveis:** studies, languages, activities, recreation, things formed by small parts, food, minerals, materials, ideas, feelings, qualities, illnesses, natural phenomena, gases.
(2) **A classificação contável/incontável**, às vezes, depende do contexto: I don't have much hair; There are two hairs in my coffee!

Exercises [answers on p. 189]

1 Complete the sentences with words from the box.

| kilos | ~~piece~~ | pieces | sheet | cartons | bottles | slice | tubes | pack |

1. He gave me a good _____ *piece* _____ of advice.
2. I bought two _____ of meat.
3. We need two _____ of vinegar and a _____ of coal.
4. They sold some _____ of furniture when they moved to LA.
5. I want just one _____ of cake, please.

6. You have to buy two _____ of toothpaste.
7. I'm going to buy four _____ of milk.
8. I need a _____ of paper to write a message.

2 Underline the uncountable nouns.

1. I want some water and three loaves of bread.
2. I don't have much money, just five dollars.
3. All we need is patience and love.
4. Don't put all the sand in one box.
5. You can light the fire with a match.
6. There's too much light here!
7. My ring is made of gold.
8. Your luggage looks heavy.

3 Check the uncountable nouns in the lists below.

1.
time	✓	hour	___	butter	___
lava	___	wood	___	box	___
cereal	___	dark	___	pack	___

2.
information	___	pieces	___	peace	___
progress	___	justice	___	education	___
school	___	wisdom	___	love	___

3.
mathematics	___	vocabulary	___	words	___
music	___	song	___	economics	___
dancing	___	soccer	___	work	___

4.
bucket	___	anger	___	beauty	___
courage	___	honesty	___	intelligence	___
patience	___	wisdom	___	bottle	___

23 Degrees of Comparison I

More/most..., ... -er/-est

Palavras como *happy, soon, happily* etc. (adjetivos e advérbios) podem ser usadas nos graus normal, comparativo e superlativo.

(positive) (comparative) (superlative)
Jim is **old**. Carl is **older than** Jean. Alex is **the oldest** of the three.
(mais velho do que) (o mais velho)

Para formar os graus comparativo e superlativo, usa-se...

1. more... / most...	2. ...-er/...-est
com palavras longas[1]:	com palavras curtas[1]:
beautiful – **more** beautiful	young – young**er**
– **most** beautiful	– young**est**
I'm **more** beautiful than you.	He's young**er** than you.
I'm the **most** beautiful girl around.	He's the young**est** man in town.

Spelling

Ao receber **-er/-est**, não há alteração na grafia da maioria das palavras:

low – low**er** – low**est**   tall – tall**er** – tall**est**   old – old**er** – old**est**

Há alteração na grafia de palavra com final:

1. -e	2. c. y[2]	3. c. v. c.[2]
perdem o -e:	muda y para i:	dobra a consoante:
late – later – latest	happy – happier – happiest	hot – hotter – hottest
safe – safer – safest	early – earlier – earliest	thin – thinner – thinnest

Notes – (1) **palavras longas** (mais de uma sílaba): intelligent, handsome etc.; **palavras curtas** (uma sílaba): new, happy, etc.; (2) **c.** = consoante; **v.** = vogal; (3) **alguns adjetivos** aceitam as duas formas (-er/est e more/most): clever, common, polite, quiet, simple, stupid, sure etc.

Exercises [answers on p. 189]

1 Underline the correct alternative.

1. My son is the (more active, <u>most active</u>) boy I know.
2. Susan is (more attractive, most attractive) than Helen.
3. This is the (more brilliant, most brilliant) diamond I've seen.
4. My mother is (more careful, most careful) than my aunt when cooking.
5. I am (more courageous, most courageous) than Pete.

2 Write the comparative and superlative forms of the words below.

1. short — *shorter* — *shortest*
2. late — _____ — _____
3. early — _____ — _____
4. narrow — _____ — _____
5. wise — _____ — _____
6. soon — _____ — _____
7. angry — _____ — _____
8. big — _____ — _____
9. heavy — _____ — _____

3 Supply the correct form of the words given.

1. My sister is _____*cleverer*_____ (clever) than my brother.
2. Grandpa drives _____ (slowly) than Grandma.
3. This is the _____ (long) road in town.
4. She is _____ (pretty) than her sister.
5. Is Alex the _____ (popular) boy at school?
6. Are dogs _____ (intelligent) than cats?
7. Are deserts _____ (beautiful) than glaciers?
8. Is Math the _____ (difficult) subject?
9. This is the _____ (hot) month of the year.

24 Degrees of Comparison II

Irregular comparison

Algumas palavras formam o **comparativo** e o **superlativo** de modo irregular.

normal	comparative	superlative
much, many	more	most
good, well	better	best
bad, badly	worse	worst
little	less	least
far	farther, further	farthest, furthest

I'm too tired to go **further**.
This book is **worse** than that.

What is the **farthest** point on land?
This is the **worst** book I've read.

Constructions

Alguns outros tipos de construção são usados em comparações.

1. not so... as /as... as (não/tão... quanto)	
He is **as** sad **as** we are.	Come **as** quickly **as** possible.
I'm **not so/as** thin **as** you.	I'm **not so/as** shy **as** you.
2. the (comparative), the (comparative) (quanto mais... melhor)	**3. (comparative) and (comparative)** (mais e mais...)
The sooner we do it, **the better**.	It is getting **colder and colder**.
The more difficult, **the worse**.	It is **more and more difficult**.

Exercises [answers on p. 190]

1 Check the correct alternative.

1. She sings well but I can sing _____ *better* _____ .
   a. better ✓   b. worst   c. good

2. Debra is the _____ person I know.
   a. worse b. worst c. bad
3. We live far but our friends live _____ .
   a. far b. farthest c. farther
4. Did you read _____ books than I did?
   a. many b. most c. more
5. My grandmother is the _____ person I know.
   a. badly b. best c. better
6. Sheila is the _____ shy person at school.
   a. less b. least c. little
7. Eating is _____ interesting than cooking.
   a. less b. little c. least
8. He was treated _____ than his sisters.
   a. worse b. worst c. best

2 Match the columns.
1. She was as busy   a. as a mouse.
2. Talk to me as soon   b. as a bird.
3. The boy was as silent   c. as a bee.
4. I feel as free   d. as a dog.
5. He was as hungry   e. as possible.

3 Complete the sentences. Use the words given.
1. The day is getting (cold) _____*colder and colder*_____ .
2. The kids are getting (bad) _____ .
3. This course is (difficult) _____ .
4. There is (little) _____ clean river water.
5. Food is (expensive) _____ .

4 Complete the sentences. Use the words given.
1. The more you buy, (much) _____*the more*_____ you want to buy.
2. The sooner we get there, (good) _____*the better*_____ .
3. The hotter, (good) _____ .
4. The more we saw, (little) _____ we could believe.
5. The more he shouted at us, (fast) _____ we ran.

25 Demonstratives and Distributives

This, that, each, every etc.

Demonstratives

This, these, that, those são demonstrativos. Funcionam como adjetivos ou pronomes:

This house is mine.
(adj.)

This is good.
(pron.)

1. para itens ou coisas próximas	2. para itens ou coisas distantes
this (este/a, isto)	**that** (aquele/a, esse/a)
these (estes/as)	**those** (aqueles/as, esses/as)
This film is very funny!	**That** man looks sad.
I must talk to you **this** week.	**That** was a bad game.
These cars are for sale.	I was happy in **those** years.

Note – **Adjetivos** acompanham substantivos; **Pronomes** substituem substantivos.

Distributives

Each, every, either, neither são distributivos; referem-se a indivíduos de um grupo. A concordância é feita com a 3ª pessoa do singular.

every (cada = todos)	**either** (qualquer dos dois)
Every girl **is** coming by car.	**Either** answer **is** correct.
each (cada = um por um)	**neither** (nenhum dos dois)
Each person **has** a number.	**Neither** girl **is** ready.

Note – **Every:** para grupos com mais de 3 itens; **each:** para grupos de 2 a 3 itens; De modo geral, **each** e **every** podem ocupar o lugar um do outro: Each / Every student is going to receive a medal.

Exercises [answers on p. 190]

1 Underline the correct demonstrative.

1. My parents lived in (<u>this</u>, these) house.
2. (This, These) book is mine, yours is (that, this).
3. Who is selling (that, those) books?
4. Why don't you buy (these, this) magazines?
5. I'm so happy! (This, That) is the best day of my life.
6. I was so happy! (This, That) was the best day of my life.
7. (Those, That) black cats jumped over the wall.
8. (This, These) are my children: John and Karen.

2 Supply the correct form of to be.

1. This ____is____ Paul. He ____is____ my best friend.
2. Where _____ those red pieces of paper?
3. These apples _____ fresh.
4. That movie _____ disgusting. I hated it!
5. Those boots _____ old but I loved them.
6. This _____ a good day to go fishing.
7. That _____ not a good day to go fishing.

3 Turn into Portuguese.

1. Neither team is going to win the championship.

2. Each hand has five fingers.

3. Either John or Serge was fired.

4 Underline the correct verb tense.

1. Every man (<u>is</u>, are) wearing a hat.
2. Each ham sandwich (has, have) two slices of bread.
3. Either road (lead, leads) to the railway station.
4. Neither Mike nor Jessica (have lived, lives) there.
5. Either of the dogs (make, makes) a good pet.
6. Every teacher (has, have) thirty students.
7. Neither chair (were, was) good.
8. Each of the men (is, are) wearing a red tie.

26 Do

Present & past

Do pode funcionar como verbo principal (= fazer) ou como verbo auxiliar (= não se traduz). Como auxiliar, ajuda o verbo principal a formar negativas, interrogativas e perguntas. Nesses casos, o verbo principal fica no infinitivo.

He **does** his job. He **doesn't** like tea. Where **did** he work?
(principal) (auxiliar) (auxiliar)

Present (affirmative)		Past (affirmative)	
I **do**	We **do**	I **did**	We **did**
You **do**	You **do**	You **did**	You **did**
He, she, it **does**	They **do**	He, she, it **did**	They **did**

Forms	
interrogative: **Do** you do …? **Does** he do …? **Did** he do …?	question: **What** do you do? **What** does he do? **What** did he do?
negative: I do **not** do … He does **not** do … He did **not** do …	short answer: Yes, **I do**. No, **I don't**. Yes, **he does**. No, **he doesn't**. Yes, **he did**. No, **he didn't**.
negative-interrogative: **Don't** you do …? **Doesn't** he do …? **Didn't** he do …?	contracted form: do not: **don't** does not: **doesn't** did not: **didn't**

Notes – interrogative: auxiliar antes do sujeito; **question:** palavra interrogativa antes do auxiliar; **negative:** auxiliar + not; **negative-interrogative:** auxiliar negativo e contraído antes do sujeito.

Exercises [answers on p. 191]

1 Answer the questions. Use short answers.

1. Do you like chocolate?   Yes, *I do.*
2. Does Rihanna sing blues?   No, _____
3. Do your friends hate you? No, _____
4. Did you wash your hands?   Yes, _____
5. Did you sing last night?   No, _____

2 Turn the sentences into the interrogative form.

1. I go to school in the morning.   *Do I go to school in the morning?*
2. My sister loves pancakes.   _____
3. The boys walk the dog in the afternoon. _____
4. My brother painted the gate yesterday.   _____
5. The workers always do their job. _____

3 Turn the sentences into the negative form.

1. We walk to school.   *We don't walk to school.*
2. Claudia goes to work by bus.   _____
3. They love science fiction.   _____
4. The students worked a lot.   _____
5. He built a dog house.   _____

4 Ask questions. Use the words given.

1. They live in Rio. (Where)
   Where do they live?
2. The boy loves his parents. (Who)
   _____
3. He studies in the afternoon. (When)
   _____
4. Ann painted the door. (What)
   _____
5. She went home. (Why)
   _____

27 Do & Make

Do e **make** (= fazer), embora tenham a mesma tradução, expressam ideias diferentes. O ideal é familiarizar-se com as expressões pois não há definições precisas.

make	do
Expressa criação, construção, preparação, planos, decisões:	Expressa execução de atividades indefinidas, deveres, lazer:
make a cake	do homework
make a dress	do a favor
make a face	do an experiment
make a fortune	do the dishes
make a mistake	do the laundry
make a phone call	do the housework
make a promise	do the cleaning
make a visit	do one's hair
make business	do one's makeup
make dinner	do a crossword
make food	do the ironing
make me nervous	do the washing
make tea	do nothing
make the bed	do everything

Exercises [answers on p. 192]

1 Write sentences. Use the words given.

1. (Who – do – a favor)
   Who did you a favor?

2. (children – make – a fire)

3. (Jeff – make – an attempt)

4. (car – do – 60 miles per hour)

5. (Dad – do – the dishes)

2 Rewrite the words under the correct heading.

a choice	a visit	friends
a comment	a work	good
a difference	a project	harm
a journey	a test	love
a mess	an effort	money
a noise	an excuse	one's best
a payment	an exception	one's nails
a plan	a reservation	one's worst
a speech	badly	the shopping
a suggestion	the cooking	well

make	do
a choice	a journey

28 Exclamatory Sentences & Other Sentence Types

Frases são usadas para formular afirmações, pedidos, questões ou para transmitir emoções como medo, surpresa, admiração etc. São classificadas de acordo com seu propósito:

1. declarative	3. imperative
(declarações)	(ordens e pedidos)
I will leave now.	Come back soon.
I didn't like the show.	Pass me the salt, please.
2. interrogative	**4. exclamatory**
(perguntas)	(sentimentos e emoções)
São finalizadas com ponto de interrogação.	São finalizadas com ponto de exclamação.
Did you see him**?**	What a wonderful garden**!**
What did he say**?**	How nice of you**!**

Exclamatory sentences geralmente contêm palavras como:

Amazing!	How joyful!	Well Done!
Awesome!	How noble of you!	What a great victory!
Bravo!	How sweet!	What a nice evening!
Brilliant!	How terrible!	What a pity!
Congratulations!	Hurrah! We've won!	What a shame!
Excellent!	Magnificent!	What a pleasant surprise!
Fantastic!	Marvellous!	What a surprise!
Hooray!	Oh!	What an idea!
How absurd!	Oh! No!	Wow!
How bad!	Ouch!	Wow, that was a thrilling ride!
How clever of you!	Ouch, that hurts!	
How disgusting!	Unbelievable!	

Exercises [answers on p. 192]

1 Classify the sentences as D (declarative), IMP (imperative), INT (interrogative) or E (exclamatory).

1.	Respond immediately.	D	(IMP)	INT	E
2.	Declarative sentences make a statement.	D	IMP	INT	E
3.	This is the best day of my life!	D	IMP	INT	E
4.	I can't wait for the party!	D	IMP	INT	E
5.	Have you had breakfast?	D	IMP	INT	E
6.	Oh, my goodness, I won!	D	IMP	INT	E
7.	The concert begins in one hour.	D	IMP	INT	E
8.	Please lower your voice.	D	IMP	INT	E
9.	What did you like best?	D	IMP	INT	E
10.	The river is rising!	D	IMP	INT	E

2 Rewrite the sentences according to the instructions.

1. a poetry contest
   (INT) *Is it a poetry contest?*
   (E) *Wow, it's a poetry contest!*
2. that magazine article
   (IMP) _____
   (IN) _____
3. a long river
   (E) _____
   (IN) _____
4. snowing
   (E) _____
   (D) _____

29 Future Tenses I

General table

Vários tempos verbais podem expressar ações futuras. Algumas vezes, a diferença entre eles é pequena ou inexistente, dependendo apenas de onde são usados.

newspaper: The headmaster **will close** the old laboratory.
oral: The headmaster **is going to close** the old laboratory.

verb tense	expresses
present simple verbo (+s/es)	ação futura fixada, marcada: My classes **start** at 8 a.m. every day. My train **leaves** at six.
present progressive be + v.-ing*	ação planejada no futuro próximo: I**'m going** to the club today. She **is seeing** Jordan at 7:00.
going to be + going to + v.	ação planejada no futuro: I**'m going to go** to the club today. She **is going to see** Jordan at 7:00.
future simple will + v.	suposição, ação não planejada, declaração de fatos, decisão no momento da fala: It **will be** a nice party. The sun **will rise** at 6:00 tomorrow.
future progressive will be + v.-ing	ação em andamento no futuro: I **will be meeting** my friends at 7 p.m. We**'ll be flying** to Paris at this time tomorrow.
future perfect will have + v. pp	ação terminada no futuro: We **will have cooked** lunch before you arrive. I**'ll have finished** this work before dinner.
future perfect progressive will have been + v.-ing	ênfase da duração da ação: He **will have been working** for 20 hours. Tomorrow, I **will have been climbing** this mountain for 5 days.

Note – *Abreviações: **v.** = verbo; **-ing** = terminação ing; **pp** = past participle.

Exercises [answers on p. 192]

1 Answer the questions. Use the words given.

1. What time will the sun rise tomorrow? (at 6:00)
   The sun will rise at six.

2. What time does the train depart? (in 10 minutes)
   _____

3. When does the meeting begin? (at 2:00)
   _____

4. When will all the students have their own computers at school? (in 2030)
   _____

5. Will they let you go with us? (No)
   _____

6. When will she come? (soon)
   _____

2 Check the correct alternative.

1. We _____ *'re going to buy* _____ a car next month.
   a. 're going to buy ✓   b. buy   c. will to

2. I think my sister _____ to the dentist tomorrow.
   a. 's going to   b. go   c. 'll go

3. I _____ to the new teacher in an hour.
   a. will has talk   b. will be talking   c. is talking

4. Susan _____ her bike next week.
   a. going to repair   b. will have repaired   c. will repaired

5. We are sure that we _____ to the university next year.
   a. will go   b. will going   c. are going

6. By the end of next week, I _____ the book.
   a. will read   b. go to read   c. will have read

30 Future Tenses II

Future simple & going to

Ambos, **Will e Going to**, são usados com expressões de tempo como: *in May, in 2020, tomorrow, tonight, next month, next year, after dinner* etc.

Will	Going to
Expressa fato futuro, previsão com base em opinião, decisão no momento da fala. The sun **will rise** tomorrow. Are you tired? I **will help** you!	Expressa previsão com base em evidência, decisão antes do momento da fala. Look, it **is going to snow**. I'**m going to work** in Miami.
Future Simple will + v. affirmative: I You He, she, it **will swim**. We You They	**Going to** be + going to + v. affirmative: I **am** You **are** He, she, it **is going to swim**. We **are** You **are** They **are**

Forms	
interrogative: **Will** he swim? **Is** he going to swim? negative: He **will not** swim. He **is not** going to swim. negative-interrogative: **Won't** he swim? **Isn't** he going to swim?	question: **Where** will he swim? **Where** is he going to swim? short answer: Yes, he **will**. No, he **won't**. Yes, he **is**. No, he **isn't**. contracted form: will: **'ll** will not: **won't** am: **'m** am not: **'m not** are: **'re** are not: **aren't** is: **'s** is not: **isn't**

Note – **negative-interrogative**: auxiliar negativo e contraído antes do sujeito.

Exercises [answers on p. 193]

1 **Rewrite the sentences in the negative form.**

1. I will make dinner.
   I won't make dinner.
2. We will meet the girls at school.

3. They are going to arrive soon.

4. He is going to spend his vacation in Rio.

2 **Rewrite the sentences in the interrogative form.**

1. It will be easy to do that.
   Will it be easy to do that?
2. You will help your friends.

3. I am going to find a new job.

4. We are going to visit her soon.

3 **Underline the correct alternative.**

1. There is no sugar! I (will, am going to) get some.
2. Ann's birthday (will be, is going) next month.
3. I (will, am going to) buy a new dress for the party.
4. The phone is ringing! I (will, am going to) get it.
5. He said he (is going to, will to) invite his new friend.
6. I don't know exactly but I think his cousins (will, are going) come.

31 Future Tenses III

Future progressive & future perfect

Future Progressive
will be + v.-ing

Indica ação em andamento no futuro:
In April, I'll be writing a book.[2]

affirmative:
He **will be writing**.
negative:
He **will not** be writing.
interrogative:
Will he be writing?

Future Perfect[*]
will have + verbo pp[1]

Indica o término de uma ação no futuro:
I'll have written the book by July.[2]

affirmative:
He **will have written** it.
negative:
He **will not** have written it.
interrogative:
Will he have written it?

Notes – **(1) pp** = particípio passado; **(2) traduções:** Em abril estarei encrevendo um livro; Terei escrito o livro até julho. *__future perfect progressive:__ will have been + v.ing. É um tempo verbal pouco usado. Enfatiza a duração da ação: By 4:00 he will have been sleeping for 20 hours.

Exercises [answers on p. 193]

1 Supply the future progressive of the verbs given.

1. (wait) I _____'ll be waiting_____ for you at the restaurant.
2. (sleep) The baby _____ after lunch.
3. (arrive) Mom _____ by 11:00.
4. (get) They _____ there at this time tomorrow.
5. (fly) We _____ home at this time next week.
6. (finish) He _____ his test by the time we arrive.
7. (study) I _____ math after dinner.
8. (read) We _____ the contract when you arrive.

2 Supply the future perfect of the verbs given.

1. (move) We _____'ll have moved_____ to Rio by July.
2. (land) The plane _____ by 5:00 p.m.

3. (sell) She _____ her car before Christmas.
4. (receive) I _____ my certificate by next January.
5. (write) He _____ his novel before the end of the month.
6. (clean) We _____ the kitchen before they arrive.
7. (bake) She _____ the cake before dinner.
8. (stop) It _____ raining before the wedding party.

3 Answer the questions.

1. What will you be doing at 5 p.m. tomorrow?

2. Will you be studying at 10 a.m. tomorrow?

3. Will you be having lunch at 12:00?

4. Will you have had dinner by 10 p.m. today?

5. What will you have done by 5 p.m. tomorrow?

4 Ask questions. Use the given information.

1. They will be studying English tomorrow at this time. (what)
   What will they be studying tomorrow at this time?

2. I will be cooking potatoes for dinner. (what)

3. Janet will be arriving by midnight. (when)

4. They will have arrived by 10:00. (what time)

5. He will have slept at Grandma's. (Where)

32 Gender of Nouns

Em inglês os substantivos são classificados como: *masculine, feminine, common and neuter* (masculino, feminino, comum e neutro).

Neuter – substantivos referentes a coisas inanimadas:
tree, car, table, fire, hospital, mountain   etc.

Common – substantivos comuns aos gêneros masculino e feminino:
teacher, student, doctor, child, friend, singer   etc.

Masculine and feminine – alguns substantivos referentes a pessoas e animais que expressam o gênero por meio de:

1. palavras diferentes	2. adição de prefixos ou sufixos
bachelor – **spinster**	actor – **actress**
boy – **girl**	baron – **baroness**
brother – **sister**	duke – **duchess**
bull – **cow**	god – **goddess**
father – **mother**	lion – **lioness**
horse – **mare**	he-bear – **she-bear**
husband – **wife**	hero – **heroine**
king – **queen**	father-in-law – **mother-in-law**
man – **woman**	
nephew – **niece**	
son – **daughter**	
uncle – **aunt**	

Exercises [answers on p. 194]

1 Complete the list below. Use words from the box.

> hostess   ~~bride~~   step-mother   nun   empress   lady   policewoman
> witch   poetess   godmother   heroine   cow   tigress   daughter-in-law

1. bridegroom   *bride*
2. poet   _____

3. godfather   _____
4. host   _____
5. friar   _____
6. gentleman   _____
7. wizard   _____
8. policeman   _____
9. emperor   _____
10. tiger   _____
11. son-in-law   _____
12. step-father   _____
13. hero   _____
14. bull   _____

2 Check the masculine form of the underlined words.

1. The Queen waved to the children from the balcony.
   a. wizard   b. King ✓   c. duke
2. The wife of my friend has got a pneumonia.
   a. husband   b. uncle   c. aunt
3. Alex is the daughter of my best friend.
   a. son   b. brother   c. bachelor
4. The nun helped the poor woman to cross the river.
   a. man   b. friar   c. he-man
5. Carly wants to be a policewoman when she grows up.
   a. policeman   b. policeboy   c. he-police
6. The princess was tired and left the room.
   a. prince   b. king   c. he-prince
7. I invited my niece for the ceremony.
   a. father-in-law   b. step-brother   c. nephew

3 Check the words common to masculine and feminine genders.

artist ✓	granddaughter	servant
baby	husband	student
bull	leader	teacher
candidate	lion	uncle
child	president	viscountess
emperor	prince	waitress
gentleman	reporter	wife

33 Gerund I

Gerund & present participle

O **Gerúndio** e o **Particípio Presente** são idênticos na forma mas diferentes no uso. Ambos são formados por **verbo + ing**: danc**ing**, do**ing**, act**ing** etc.

Gerund É usado:	Present Participle É usado:
como substantivo. **Running** is a good exercise. **Dancing** is my pastime. No **smoking** here.	como adjetivo. That was an **amazing** evening. It is an **interesting** idea.
depois de preposições. She is good **at painting**. I left **without saying** a word.	em tempos contínuos. I **am writing**. She **was sleeping**.
depois de certos verbos e expressões.[1] I **hate swimming**. It's no use **helping** her.	depois de verbos de percepção. I **saw** him **running**. I **smell** something **burning**. He **felt** the house **shaking**.

Spelling

Ao receber **-ing** não há alteração na grafia da maioria dos verbos:

drink**ing**   do**ing**   go**ing**   teach**ing**   sing**ing**   paint**ing**   etc.

Mas, verbo terminado em...

| 1. e:
perde o e
hav**e** – hav**ing**
tak**e** – tak**ing**
exceto: s**ee**ing, agr**ee**ing | 2. ie:
muda para y
d**ie** – d**y**ing
t**ie** – t**y**ing | 3. c.v.c.[2] (sílaba tônica):
dobra a consoante
hi**t** – hi**tt**ing
cu**t** – cu**tt**ing
exceto: gro**w**ing, mi**x**ing |

Notes – **(1) Verbos/expressões** seguidos por gerúndio: admit, like, dislike, hate, enjoy, imagine, finish, keep, can't stand etc. **(2) c.v.c. =** consoante, vogal, consoante.

Exercises [answers on p. 195]

1 Supply the gerund form of the verbs given.

1. (wait) It's no use _waiting_ for him.
2. (be) He can't stand _____ close to her.
3. (see) I'm looking forward to _____ you soon.
4. (go) Do you mind _____ to the next counter?
5. (paint) He is good at _____.
6. (exceed) I was fined for _____ the speed limit.
7. (write) Please, keep on _____.
8. (drive) _____ makes me nervous.
9. (step) The sign says: "No _____ on the grass."
10. (cook) My _____ is famous around here.

2 Supply the present participle of the verbs given.

1. (relax) This is a very _relaxing_ activity.
2. (make) He is _____ progress at the moment.
3. (live) I think the Watsons are _____ abroad.
4. (run) The girls are not _____ in the park.
5. (swim) Kevin is _____ in the lake.
6. (lie) I believe the boys are _____.
7. (sing) I heard someone _____ this morning.
8. (burn) There was nobody inside the _____ house.
9. (smile) The _____ boy attracted our attention.
10. (get) They left without _____ their money.

3 Classify the underlined words as G (for Gerund) or P (for Present Participle).

1. Fishing is fun. (G) P
2. This is a very interesting idea. G P
3. Is grandma watching TV? G P
4. Who is writing the message? G P
5. She is an amazing woman. G P
6. Water-skiing is a dangerous sport. G P
7. Grandma hates cooking. G P
8. The crying baby was terribly cold. G P
9. We like driving to the mountains. G P

34 Gerund II

Verbs followed by gerund/infinitive – list

Verbs Followed by Gerund	
admit	He admitted **being** late.
advise	Doctors usually advise **eating** fruit.
allow	They don't allow **talking** inside here.
appreciate	We appreciate her **talking** to us.
avoid	They avoided **making** mistakes.
begin[1]	He began **teaching** children.
be worth	It is worth **listening** to him.
be no use	It's no use **waiting** for her.
can't help	I can't help **laughing** in class.
complete	He completed **restoring** the statue.
confess	They confessed **being** guilty.
consider	I considered **buying** a new house.
continue[1]	He continued **studying**.
delay	He delayed **sending** the letter.
deny	She denied **committing** the crime.
detest	We detest **walking** to the office.
dislike	They dislike **wearing** those shoes.
enjoy	I enjoy **going** to the beach.
fear	He fears **being** by himself.
feel like	I feel like **going** to the movies.
finish	He finished **writing** his report.
forget	He forgot **locking** the car.
hate[1]	I hate **eating** vegetables.
imagine	I imagined **moving** to the seaside.
keep	He keeps **visiting** me.
like[1]	He likes **swimming**.
love	I love **going** to the beach.
mind	I don't mind **waiting** for them.
miss	She misses **talking** to him in the morning.
permit	They don't permit **smoking** here.

Note – (1) Gerund/Infinitive *sem mudança de significado*.

postpone	She postponed **returning** to Liverpool.
practice	They practiced **playing** tennis yesterday.
prefer	We prefer **reading** fiction.
prevent	We prevented her from **breaking** her leg.
propose	He proposed **staying** home.
quit	I quit **smoking** ten years ago.
recall	She recalled **having** closed the door before leaving.
report	He reported her **helping** the students.
resent	We resented **spending** so much time with him.
resist	He resisted **eating** the slice of cake.
risk	He risked **getting** fired.
start	It started **raining**.
suggest	I suggested her **taking** a rest.
tolerate	I tolerate his **singing** that song.
understand	We understand his **leaving** earlier.

Note – (1) Gerund/Infinitive sem mudança de significado.

Verbs Followed by Gerund or Infinitive[2]	
forget	I forgot **to meet** him. (esqueceu de ir ao encontro) I forgot **meeting** him. (não se lembra de ter encontrado)
go on	He went on **to learn** English. (continuou para poder aprender) He went on **learning** English. (continuou aprendendo)
quit	She quit **to work** here. (deixou outro trabalho para trabalhar aqui) She quit **working**. (deixou de trabalhar)
remember	She remembered **to visit** me. (lembrou de visitar) She remembered **visiting** me. (lembrou da visita feita)
stop	He stopped **to smoke**. (parou para fumar) He stopped **smoking**. (parou de fumar)

Note – (2) Gerund/Infinitive com mudança de significado.

Have

Present & past

To have pode ser usado como verbo principal ou auxiliar. Como principal pode indicar posse (= ter) ou ter o significado de *take* e *give*. Como auxiliar ajuda na construção de *perfect tenses*.

She **has** black hair.

(principal)

We **had** a party.

(principal)

They **have** seen you.

(auxiliar)

Present (affirmative)	Past (affirmative)	
I **have**	I	
You **have**	You	
He/She/It **has**	He/she/it	**had**
They **have**	They	
We **have**	We	

Forms*	
interrogative:	**question:**
Have you...?	**Where** have you...?
Has he...?	**What** has he...?
Had he...?	**Where** had he...?
negative:	**short answer:**
I have **not**...	Yes, **I have**. No, **I haven't**.
He has **not**...	Yes, **he has**. No, **he hasn't**.
He had **not**...	Yes, **he had**. No, **he hadn't**.
negative-interrogative:	**contracted form:**
Haven't you...?	have: **'ve** have not: **haven't**
Hasn't he...?	has: **'s** has not: **hasn't**
Hadn't he...?	had: **'d** had not: **hadn't**

Note – *é comum o uso do auxiliar **do** para formar as interrogativas e negativas de **have** como verbo principal: I don't have; He doesn't have; He didn't have; Do you have?; Does he have?; Did he have?

Exercises [answers on p. 195]

1 **Classify the underlined verbs as P (principal) or A (auxiliary).**

1. My friends <u>have</u> a beautiful house by the lake.   (P)   A
2. Those girls <u>have</u> lived in Toronto.   P   A
3. My sister <u>has</u> a little dog.   P   A
4. I <u>had</u> a terrible cold last month.   P   A
5. They <u>had</u> dinner at 7:00 p.m.   P   A
6. They <u>had</u> had dinner when I arrived.   P   A
7. That woman <u>has</u> three children.   P   A
8. <u>Has</u> Alex arrived yet?   P   A
9. I <u>have</u> worked hard.   P   A

2 **Check the correct alternative.**

1. I _____ two new books.
      a. hasn't   b. has   c. have ✓
2. Bob _____ a tall brother.
      a. has   b. have   c. haven't
3. We _____ two English classes last week.
      a. had   b. have   c. has
4. Mom _____ a headache yesterday.
      a. has   b. have   c. had
5. That water _____ a bad taste.
      a. haven't   b. has   c. have
6. The Brazilian flag _____ four colors.
      a. had   b. has   c. have
7. My father _____ an old car last year.
      a. has   b. have   c. had
8. He _____ a new car today.
      a. had   b. has   c. haven't
9. What time does your best friend _____ dinner?
      a. have   b. has   c. had

36 Have II

Causative form

Causative forms são usadas para expressar ações feitas por nossa causa, a nosso pedido, para nós. Os verbos *have, get* e *make* são comuns nesse tipo de construção.

I **had/got** my car polished.
(Mandei polir/Poli meu carro.)

I **had/made** them cook lunch.
(Mandei/Fiz com que preparassem o almoço.)

Forms	
1. to have something done (have + objeto + v. pp[1]) She **had** the car **washed**. They **had** their house **painted**.	**2. to have someone do something** (have + agente + infinitivo s/ to) I **had** John **fix** the car. I **had** the boys **cook** dinner.

Verb tenses	
Present Simple	I **have** my car washed often.
Past Simple	I **had** my hair cut yesterday.
Future Simple	I'**ll have** my car fixed. I'**m going** to have my car sold.
Present Progressive	I'**m having** my hair done.
Past Progressive	I **was having** the garage repaired.
Future Progressive	I'**ll be having** the swimming pool cleaned.
Present Perfect	I **have had** the door fixed.
Past Perfect	I **had had** the alarm system installed.
Future Perfect	I **will have had** the house sold.
Modal Verbs: must, can etc.	We **must have** a pizza delivered.

Notes – (1) pp = past participle; **obs.: as formas negativas, interrogativas e questões** são feitas por verbos auxiliares: They didn't have the house painted; Did you have your hair cut?; Where do you have your car fixed?

Exercises [answers on p. 195]

1 Check the correct alternative.

1. You can have your watch _____ at a jeweler.
   a. stolen   b. cut   c. repaired ✓
2. You'll have a mechanic _____ it.
   a. stolen   b. fixed   c. repair
3. I'm going to have Tom _____ dinner.
   a. cook   b. burned   c. eaten
4. We'll have our photos _____ for the passports.
   a. taken   b. take   c. get
5. She had her assistant _____ the report.
   a. typing   b. type   c. types
6. I'm having my house _____ right now.
   a. vacuum   b. polish   c. cleaned
7. She had her bedroom _____ last year.
   a. redecorate   b. redecorated   c. build
8. He'll have his lawyer _____ into it.
   a. looked   b. 'll look   c. look

2 Rewrite the sentences. Use causative forms.

1. She polishes her shoes.
   She has her shoes polished.
2. He watered the garden.

3. He is mending his car.

4. She was cutting her hair.

5. We will repair the roof.

6. I have cleaned the windows.

7. He had ironed his clothes.

8. He may send the box.

37 How & compounds

How (como, de que maneira, por qual razão) pode ser usado na formulação de perguntas.

How do you cook beans? **How** does he look like? **How** is she?
How do you know it? **How** about going home? **How** did you like it?

Compounds

Em conjunto com outras palavras **How** adquire novos significados.

How big (Qual o tamanho): **How big** is that box?	**How many** (Quantos): **How many** cars do you have?
How deep (Qual a profundidade): **How deep** is the lake?	**How much** (Quanto): **How much** does it cost?
How far (Qual a distância): **How far** is it from here?	**How often** (Qual a frequência): **How often** does it rain here?
How fast (Qual a velocidade): **How fast** can you run?	**How old** (Quantos anos): **How old** is this castle?
How heavy (Qual o peso): **How heavy** is that chair?	**How tall** (Qual a altura - pessoas): **How tall** is your brother?
How high (Qual a altura): **How high** is Sugar Loaf?	**How well** (Quão bem): **How well** does he cook?
How long (Qual o tempo/medida): **How long** did you work there? **How long** is the road to L.A.?	**How wide** (Qual a largura): **How wide** is the bridge?

[Ver Wh- questions, p. 171]

Exercises [answers on p. 196]

1 Match the columns.

1. How often do you go shopping?   ____   a.   I like it a lot!
2. How many sisters do you have?   ____   b.   About $20.
3. How long is this river?   _1_   c.   Every week.

4. How heavy is that box? _____ d. I'm fine.
5. How much does that book cost? _____ e. Ten kilometers, I think.
6. How are you today? _____ f. About 70 pounds.
7. How old are you? _____ g. Only two.
8. How do you like your job? _____ h. I'm 21.

2 Complete the dialogs with words from the box.

> how long   ~~how~~   how fast   how wide
> how high   how deep   how heavy   how big

1. — *How* do they drive?
   — They drive fast.
2. — _____ does it take you to go to school?
   — It takes about 30 minutes.
3. — _____ is Mount Everest?
   — It is 8,848 meters high.
4. — _____ is a blue whale?
   — The blue whale can weigh up to 172 tons.
5. — _____ is the weather like today?
   — It's hot and sunny.
6. — _____ is lake Baikal in Siberia?
   — It is 1,637 meters deep.
7. — _____ is the universe?
   — Scientists can't put a number on it.
8. — _____ is 9 de Julio Avenue in Buenos Aires?
   — It has seven lanes in each direction.

3 Answer the questions about yourself.

1. How old are you?

2. How tall are you?

3. How do you go to school/work every day?

4. How do you feel today?

38 Imperative

O **imperativo** é um modo verbal usado para expressar ordem, comando, proibição, permissão, conselho, pedido ou oferecimento.

Please **stay** there!	**Turn** right!	**Don't cross** the street.
Have some tea.	**Mind** the steps.	**Turn** off the radio, please.

Dependendo da situação, aconselha-se o uso de formas menos diretas.

"Stop!" → "I have to ask you to stop."
"Stay there!" → "Could you stay there for a moment?"

Forms	
1. verbo no infinitivo sem to	**2. Let us + verbo**
affirmative:	affirmative:
Go!	**Let's** do it!
negative:	negative:
Don't go!	Let's **not** do it!

O sujeito (you) fica subentendido: **(You)** Come here!

Algumas vezes, a pessoa a quem o comando é dirigido pode aparecer no início ou no final da frase:

Jane, stand up.   **Boys**, stay here.
Get your books, **girls**.   Go to the board, **Tom**.

Exercises [answers on p. 196]

1 Write a command to each situation.

> Write it down.   Let's eat something.   Let's not leave now.
> Don't open the window.   ~~Brush your teeth.~~   Wash your hands.
> Water the flowers.   Let's not stay here.

1. The kids have had lunch.   _Brush your teeth._
2. The girls are going to have dinner. _____
3. We are hungry.   _____
4. There's too much noise in here.   _____
5. The lecture is very interesting.   _____
6. Mom planted new flowers.   _____
7. It's very cold outside.   _____
8. I don't have your phone number.   _____

2 Choose a command to each situation.

> ~~Let's visit her!~~   Do not disturb.   Do some exercise.   Behave yourself!
> Keep calm.   Have some water.   Use mine!   Take the first left.

1. Grandma is ill.   _Let's visit her!_
2. I am studying.   _____
3. I am thirsty.   _____
4. I want to lose weight!   _____
5. I'm leaving, Mom.   _____
6. It is going to be a difficult test!   _____
7. Oh, my cell phone is out of order.   _____
8. I don't know where the bank is.   _____

3 Use the imperative to complete the dialogs.

1. — Where is the drugstore?   — _____
2. — The coffee is delicious!   — _____
3. — It's a rainy afternoon!   — _____
4. — Is the baby sleeping?   — _____
5. — It's a nice, sunny day!   — _____

39 Indefinites I

Some, any, no, none

Some, any, no, none são usados quando desejamos nos referir a pessoas, coisas ou lugares de maneira vaga, indefinida. Podem funcionar como adjetivos ou pronomes.

I have **some** money.   He doesn't have **any**.
(adj.)   (pron.)

Observe o uso ...

1. Some (algum/a, alguns/mas)

em frase afirmativa:
I've bought **some** flowers.

em espera por resposta positiva:
Would you like **some** tea?

2. No, None (nenhum/a)

para dar sentido negativo:
adj.: She has **no** shoes.
pron.: He has **none**.

3. Any (algum/a, alguns/mas)

em frase interrogativa:
Do you have **any** good idea?

em frase negativa:
He didn't have **any** money.

com palavra de sentido negativo[1]:
She never eats[2] **any** meat.

com o significado de 'qualquer':
Choose **any** seat.

em orações condicionais:
If you have **any** doubt, call me.

Notes – (1) Palavras de sentido negativo: seldom, rarely, scarcely, never, without, barely etc.; (2) O verbo fica na forma afirmativa quando usado com palavras de sentido negativo.

Exercises [answers on p. 197]

1 Check the correct alternative.

1. There are _____*some*_____ beautiful spots around here.
   a. none   b. some ✓   c. any
2. They aren't hungry. They want _____ food.
   a. any   b. none   c. no
3. I need _____ fresh carrots for the soup.
   a. some   b. none   c. any

4. "Is there _____ tea left?" "Sorry, there isn't _____."
   a. no - no   b. some - some   c. any - any
5. Was there _____ problem with the car?
   a. some   b. any   c. none
6. I have _____ time to talk to you. I'm sorry.
   a. no   b. some   c. any
7. If you see _____ of the girls, tell me.
   a. any   b. no   c. some
8. We haven't had _____ news about him.
   a. some   b. any   c. no

2 Complete the sentences with the correct indefinites.
1. Take _____*any*_____ dress you like. They all suit you.
2. Do you need _____ money?
3. No, I need _____ money.
4. No, I need _____.
5. They seldom ask _____ question.
6. He left without _____ money.
7. Would you like _____ coffee?
8. We don't have _____ children.

3 Transform the sentences. Give them a positive meaning.
1. There is no money in my pocket.
   There is some money in my pocket.
2. He doesn't have any shoes.

3. She bought no books.

4. We never drink any coffee.

5. I seldom buy any magazines.

6. I arrived without any good news.

7. She doesn't do any housework.

8. I don't have any good ideas.

Indefinites II

Compounds

Os **indefinidos compostos** (Indefinite Compounds) funcionam como pronomes. Seguem as mesmas regras de uso de **some**, **any** e **no**.

Compounds	Examples
Some some**one**/some**body** (alguém) some**thing** (algo) some**where** (algum lugar)	**Some** There is **somebody** home. There is **something** wrong here. My bag is **somewhere** in this room.
No no **one**/no**body** (ninguém) no**thing** (nada) no**where** (nenhum lugar)	**No** There is **nobody** home. There's **nothing** wrong here. My bag is **nowhere** in this room.
Any any**one**/any**body** (alguém, ninguém, qualquer um) any**thing** (algo, nada, qualquer um) any**where** (algum/nenhum lugar, qualquer um)	**Any** Is there **anybody** home? Is there **anything** wrong here? Is my bag **anywhere** in this room?

Exercises [answers on p. 197]

1 Underline the correct alternative.

1. Is there (<u>anything</u>, somebody) you want to ask me?
2. (Nobody, Anything) believes him. He's a liar.
3. Will (anybody, anywhere) help us, please?
4. Don't you have (nobody, anything) to do?
5. Let's go (something, somewhere) cool tonight.

6. We must do (something, nowhere) to help her.
7. I'm cooking (anybody, something) for lunch.
8. Dad said you are going (nowhere, something)!

2 Complete the sentences. Use compounds of *some* and *any*.
1. Can _____*someone*_____ tell me where he is?
2. We spent the night _____ near the lake.
3. Don't worry about me. I can bear _____ .
4. _____ is ringing the bell!
5. I haven't seen _____ there.
6. I will try to think of _____ to tell her.
7. We don't need _____ from the market.

3 Complete the sentences. Use compounds of *no* and *any*.
1. The house is empty. _____*Nobody*_____ lives there!
2. I can see _____ without my glasses.
3. I can't hear _____ without my ear phones.
4. Invite _____ you want.
5. Does he have _____ to tell us?
6. No, I want _____ to drink, thanks.
7. Did you see my keys _____ ?

4 Complete the sentences. Use: some, any, no and compounds.
1. Is there _____*anybody*_____ waiting for us?
2. No, there's _____ waiting for us.
3. Please, don't leave _____ out of its place.
4. There are _____ students outside.
5. Did you go _____ last night?
6. There is _____ sugar in the pot.
7. _____ left his umbrella on the bus.

41 Infinitive I

Characteristics

O **infinitivo** é formado por **to + verbo**. Pode funcionar como sujeito, objeto ou complemento da oração. A forma negativa é feita com **not**.

To dance is exciting.
The best thing is **to love**.

I want **to leave** now.
I decided **not** to go.

O infinitivo pode ser usado **com** ou **sem to**.

1. O infinitivo com to é usado	2. O infinitivo sem to é usado
após certos substantivos[1]: His attempt **to move**, failed.	após except e but (exceto): I could do nothing but **weep**.
após to be + adjetivo: I'm happy **to know** you.	após would rather e had better: I'd rather **be** with you. (Prefiro...) He'd better **be** silent. (É melhor...)
para indicar finalidade: He used it **to open** the door.	após let, make, do, auxiliares modais e verbos de percepção[3]: can may will shall must could might would should feel hear notice see watch etc.
após certas expressões e verbos[2]: ask decide forget help invite learn like offer plan seem teach tell want wish the first how when where what etc.	

Notes – **(1)** geralmente substantivos abstratos; **(2) Infinitivo com to:** ver lista na p. 91; **(3) verbos de percepção:** podem ser seguidos por Gerúndio ou Infinitivo sem to.

Exercises [answers on p. 198]

1 Complete the sentences with words from the box.

fall   climb   go   ~~sing~~   cook   help   run   stay

1. He should _____ *sing* _____ a song.
2. She will _____ something for dinner.

3. I saw the cat _____ up the wall.
4. He did everything except _____ .
5. I couldn't do anything but _____ there.
6. We could _____ fast when we were young.
7. We might _____ to Africa this summer.
8. She felt the rain _____ on her face.

2 Complete the sentences with words from the box.

| ~~to open~~   to answer   to sing   to run   to see   to start   to arrive   to go |

1. I used the key _____ *to open* _____ the box.
2. He was the first _____ away.
3. She wanted _____ my questions.
4. He told us where _____ .
5. They invited us _____ at his birthday party.
6. I was the second _____ .
7. I didn't know when _____ .
8. He was glad _____ us.

3 Check the correct alternative.
1. There is no reason _____ in bed.
   a. stay   b. to stay ✓   c. buy
2. She was ready _____ when we arrived.
   a. study   b. to leave   c. leave
3. You make me _____ .
   a. laugh   b. to laugh   c. to cry
4. I must _____ my report right now.
   a. to write   b. write   c. to read
5. I saw her _____ .
   a. to cry   b. to die   c. cry
6. You had better _____ up your room.
   a. clean   b. to polish   c. dirty
7. Her favorite fantasy is _____ basketball.
   a. to play   b. to run   c. play
8. You will have a chance _____ out all water sports.
   a. try   b. to try   c. play

42 Infinitive II

Infinitive with to – list

Verbs followed by infinitive with to	
agree	They agreed **to help** us.
appear	He appears **to be** busy tomorrow.
arrange	We arranged **to spend** the weekend on the beach.
ask	She asked **to leave** before lunch.
be able	She is able **to teach** them.
beg	He begged **to be** promoted.
begin*	He began **to talk**.
can't bear*	He can't bear **to stay** alone.
care	Did he care **to walk** home?
choose	I chose **to ignore** her.
claim	He claims **to be** honest.
continue*	He continued **to study**.
dare	They won't dare **to break** the rules.
decide	I decided not **to move**.
demand	They demand **to talk** to the coach about the team.
deserve	You deserve **to be** fired!
expect	We expect **to see** her soon.
fail	He failed **to finish** the test on time.
forget*	I forgot **to close** the windows before I left home.
hate*	I hate **to feel** cold.
hesitate	She hesitated **to tell** us about her marriage.
hope	We hope **to see** you back.
intend	He intended **to answer** all the questions.
learn	He learned **to swim** when he was a baby.
like*	I like **to stay** home on rainy days.
love*	He loves **to drive** to the beach.
manage	We managed **to finish** the work on time.
mean	I didn't mean **to hurt** you.
need*	You need **to be** home before 10:00 p.m.
offer	He offered **to teach** us some English.

* Infinitive or Gerund.

plan	I'm planning **to visit** Nepal.
prefer*	We prefer **to wait** for you here.
prepare	He is preparing **to move** as soon as possible.
pretend	He pretended **to love** her.
promise	She promised **to see** us next weekend.
refuse	They refused **to leave** the room without her.
regret*	I regret **to tell** you that he won't give the lecture.
remember*	He didn't remember **to water** the flowers.
seem	She seems **to be** very frightened.
start*	He started **to shout** at us.
stop*	He stopped **to smoke**.
struggle	The boy struggled **to be** concentrated.
swear	I swear **to tell** the truth.
try*	He tried **to save** her but it was too late.
volunteer	He volunteered **to help** us with the math lesson.
wait	He waited **to talk** to the manager.
want	Do you want **to follow** us?
wish	I wish **to go** to Paris some day.

* Infinitive or Gerund.

Nouns followed by Infinitive with to		
The decision **to increase** taxes is not very popular.		
advice	order	reminder
command	permission	request
decision	plan	requirement
desire	possibility	suggestion
fact	proposal	tendency
opportunity	refusal	wish

Adjectives followed by infinitive with to		
He was determined **to win** the elections.		
amazed	disappointed	proud
anxious	eager	ready
ashamed	glad	sad
careful	happy	shocked
certain	likely	sorry
content	lucky	surprised
delighted	pleased	upset

43 Linking Verbs

Be (ser, estar), **become** (tornar-se) e **seem** (parecer) são sempre verbos de ligação. Expressam estado de ser e são seguidos por substantivos ou adjetivos.

    She **is** a teacher.   He **became** rich.   You **seem** upset.

Também podem funcionar como verbos de ligação:
→ verbos dos sentidos:

feel	**look**	**smell**	**sound**	**taste**
(sentir-se)	(parecer)	(ter cheiro)	(ter som)	(ter gosto)

→ alguns outros verbos:

appear	**get**	**grow**	**keep**	**make**	**seem**	**turn**	**remain**
(parecer)	(ficar)	(ficar)	(ficar)	(tornar)	(parecer)	(tornar-se)	(permanecer)

Action verbs

Esses mesmos verbos podem funcionar como verbos de ação; nesse caso, mudam de significado e são seguidos por substantivos ou advérbios.

	linking verbs	action verbs
appear	Peter **appears** snobbish.	He **appeared** there before lunch.
feel	I **feel** good.	This fabric **feels** lovely.
get	They **got** tired.	Have you **got** a new car?
grow	We are **growing** old.	The gardener **grows** red roses.
keep	**Keep** quiet, please.	He **kept** the book under his pillow.
make	You **make** me happy.	She **made** a chocolate cake.
look	He **looked** angry.	He **looked** angrily at us.
remain	I **remained** silent.	Mom asked us to **remain** here.
smell	The cake **smells** good.	The dog **smelled** the bone slowly.
sound	My stereo **sounds** bad.	He **sounded** the patient's chest.
stay	The kids **stay** united.	He **stayed** in the army for years.
taste	The fish **tastes** awful.	Jerry **tasted** the food carefully.
turn	She **turned** pale.	We can't **turn** our backs to reality.

Exercises [answers on p. 198]

1 Underline the correct verb to complete the sentence.

1. The beef stew dinner (<u>tasted</u>, sounded) delicious.
2. The beef stew (turned, looked) delicious.
3. The children (sounded, became) quiet.
4. "(Stay, grow) clean," she said to the children.
5. Gandhi (appeared, became) a main figure in Indian history.
6. The woman (made, looked) angry.
7. I (grew, felt) totally disappointed.
8. He (remained, felt) old.
9. The worker (appeared, smelled) tired.
10. They (looked, made) determined after the talk.

2 Underline the linking verbs.

1. I <u>became</u> the president of the student council.
2. I felt warm by the fireplace.
3. Your kids grow taller every day.
4. The food from the picnic smelled rotten.
5. Mom smelled the flowers she had received.
6. The fish tasted salty.
7. Dad tasted the fish.
8. The fruit looked fresh at the stand.
9. The firefighter sounded the emergency alarm.
10. The Queen appeared in the doorway.

3 Classify the underlined verb as L (linking) or A (action verb).

		L	A
1.	His painting remained on display for a month.	L	(A)
2.	He looked smilingly at the students.	L	A
3.	This cake tastes nice.	L	A
4.	Mary seems to like the house.	L	A
5.	I looked at all the questions on the test.	L	A
6.	The dog turned happy.	L	A
7.	The farmer grew tomatoes last season.	L	A
8.	He asked me to feel the soil under my feet.	L	A
9.	He feels he must resign.	L	A
10.	The man turned green near the waterfall.	L	A

44 Modal Auxiliaries I

Characteristics

Auxiliares Modais são um tipo de verbo auxiliar. Ajudam o verbo principal a expressar conceitos como habilidade, possibilidade, necessidade etc.

São auxiliares modais:

can/could   may/might   must   will/would
shall/should   ought to[1]   need[2] dare

Um auxiliar modal:

não tem infinitivo can may	**short form** cannot: **can't** could not: **couldn't**
não tem todos os tempos verbais could might	may not: — might not: **mightn't** must not: **mustn't**
não muda de forma: I, he, …, they **can**.	will, shall: **'ll** will not: **won't**
faz a própria negativa: I can**not**… He may **not**… etc.	would not: **wouldn't** shall not: **shan't**
faz a própria interrogativa: **Can** you…? **May** she…? etc.	should not: **shouldn't** ought not: **oughtn't**
é seguido por infinitivo sem to: I can **swim**. We may **run**. etc	

Notes – **(1) Ought to** não é usado em interrogativas; **(2) need** e **dare** podem ser **common** ou **modal verbs**: Does he need to see a doctor; Need I pay now?. He doesn't dare to interrupt me; She daren't say a word.

Exercises [answers on p. 199]

1 Check the best answer.

1. Shall I close the door?
    a. Yes, please. ✓   b. No, you don't.

2. May I board the plane?
   a. Yes, you will.   b. Yes, you may board now.
3. When should we be there?
   a. You should arrive early.   b. No, don't do that!
4. Would you like tea or coffee?
   a. I'd like tea, please.   b. I won't!
5. Must he leave now?
   a. Yes, it's an emergency.   b. Yes, he does.
6. Would you come here?
   a. Sure!   b. Yes, I can.
7. Could Dad play golf well?
   a. No, he didn't.   b. No, he couldn't.
8. Can they speak many languages?
   a. No, they wouldn't.   b. Yes, they can.

2 Match the columns.

1. Where would you like to have dinner?   _____ a. Tomorrow.
2. When can you start?   _____ b. Tom can.
3. Why should we call her?   _____ c. Because she's sad.
4. Who can teach us?   __1__ d. At the Ritz.
5. What time shall they leave?   _____ e. At five.

3 Turn the sentences into the interrogative form.

1. I may see your driver's license.
   May I see your driver's license ?
2. She will drive the car.
   _____ ?
3. You could help me move the sofa.
   _____ ?
4. He should see a doctor.
   _____ ?
5. We must talk to him.
   _____ ?

45 Modal Auxiliaries II

Meaning

Cada modal atribui um significado ao verbo principal. Observe:

You **can** leave now.   You **should** leave now.   You **must** leave now!
 (permissão)   (conselho)   (obrigação)

Para expressar tempos verbais que os modais não possuem, usamos algumas outras formas: *to be able to, to be allowed to, to have to, to be supposed to.*

I **can** dance.   I **was able to** dance.   I'**ll be able to** dance.
 (pres.)   (past)   (fut.)

Modal	Meaning
can, could (poder) to be able to	capacidade, habilidade, possibilidade, proibição, dedução: I **can** drive. He **can** swim well. I **could** teach you. You **can't** go. She **could** be tired.
may, might (poder) to be allowed to	permissão, possibilidade, dedução: You **may** go. It **might** rain. She **may** be tired.
must (dever) to have to	obrigação, proibição, dedução: I **must** study. You **mustn't** talk here. You **must** be tired.
will, shall; would to be supposed to	intenção, expectativa; pedido polido, oferecimento: I **will/shall** meet you at school. **Would** you like some coffee?
should, ought to (precisar)	opinião, conselho: He **should** see her. You **ought to** go by car.

Note – a tradução para **will** e **shall** depende do verbo principal.

Exercises [answers on p. 199]

1 Underline the meaning expressed by the modal verb.

1. They say it may snow tomorrow. (<u>possibility</u>, ability)
2. May I look at the questions now? (permission, advice)
3. It's snowing, so it must be very cold outside. (intention, deduction)
4. He must be French. (obligation, deduction)
5. I could speak German when I was seven. (ability, obligation)
6. I can't lift that suitcase by myself. (request, ability)
7. He must take his medicine three times a day. (intention, obligation)
8. That can't be the right answer. (deduction, polite request)
9. It might rain tonight. (possibility, ability)
10. You shouldn't suffer in silence. (permission, advice)
11. You mustn't step on the grass. (possibility, prohibition)
12. John could have missed the train. (intention, deduction)
13. Would you close the door, please? (polite request, obligation)
14. I shall close the door for you. (intention, obligation)
15. You ought to go to school right now. (advice, request)

2 Check the sentence with a similar meaning.

1. He can offer you the best price.
   a. He is able to offer you the best price. ✓
   b. He was able to offer the best price. _____
2. You may go to the picnic.
   a. We were allowed to go to the picnic. _____
   b. We are allowed to go to the picnic. _____
3. He must help his father repair the car.
   a. He has to help his father repair the car. _____
   b. He will have to help his father repair the car. _____
4. I will meet her at four.
   a. I am supposed to meet her at four. _____
   b. I was supposed to have met her at four. _____
5. I could get in to see the film.
   a. I was able to get in to see the film. _____
   b. I will be able to get in to see the film. _____

46 Mood

Modo é a forma assumida pelo verbo na expressão de um pensamento. São quatro os modos em inglês: indicativo, imperativo, infinitivo e subjuntivo. Observe o que cada modo expressa.

1. indicative mood	3. infinitive mood
alegação, negação, questão: (quase tudo o que escrevemos) I **work** in the morning. I **don't like** it. **Do** you **like** tea?	com características de substantivo, é conhecido como 'forma nominal do verbo' **To err** is human. I came **to see** you.
2. imperative mood	4. subjunctive mood
comando, pedido, conselho: **Open** your books. **Come** back soon. **Don't close** the door!	dúvida, desejo, condição: I ordered that Karl **paint** the walls. God **save** the Queen. I wish Ann **were** here. It is vital that he **be** here.

Subjunctive Mood

Form → subjunctive present (v. sem to): **add, think, be**
subjunctive past (= past simple): **added, thought, were**

No inglês moderno o modo subjuntivo tem sido substituído pelo modo indicativo e auxiliares modais. Porém, vale a pena saber:

O subjuntivo é usado depois de alguns verbos (+ that):	O subjuntivo é usado depois de algumas expressões (It is... that):
advise ask demand desire insist suggest urge wish etc. I **insist that** Mr. Seynor **leave** soon.	best crucial desirable important recommended vital good idea etc. It **is essential that** we **be** there.

Note – Subjuntivo negativo (not + verbo): He asked that you **not accept** the money.

Exercises [answers on p. 200]

❶ Classify the sentences as I (indicative), IMP (imperative) or S (subjunctive mood).

1. Joe, pick up the boxes.   I   (IMP)   S
2. Joe picks up the boxes.   I   IMP   S
3. I order that Joe pick up the boxes.   I   IMP   S
4. Sue is studying in her room.   I   IMP   S
5. It is essential that Sue study in her room.   I   IMP   S
6. Sue, study in your room.   I   IMP   S
7. Josh closes the windows.   I   IMP   S
8. We never go to the beach on Mondays.   I   IMP   S
9. Don't make mistakes!   I   IMP   S
10. I finished the work yesterday.   I   IMP   S

❷ Write a command to each situation.

1. The girls are not playing the guitar.
   Play the guitar, girls.
2. I am not reading my book.
   _____
3. Sheila didn't cook dinner.
   _____
4. The boys don't want to walk home.
   _____
5. The kids are shouting.
   _____

❸ Fill in the blanks. Use the verbs given.

1. (study) I suggest that he _____ *study* _____ .
2. (play) I insist that Lee _____ the guitar.
3. (begin) It is imperative that the game _____ at once.
4. (be) Is it essential that we _____ there?
5. (paint) I ask that Mark _____ the fence.
6. (guard) It was essential that Johan _____ the box.
7. (be) I wish he _____ still alive.
8. (be) If I _____ there, I would paint the fence.
9. (be) The teacher insists that her students _____ on time.
10. (be) I wish that this book _____ still in print.

47 Nouns I

Characteristics

Substantivos nomeiam pessoas, coisas, animais, locais, sentimentos etc.

woman   flower   dog   house   love

São classificados segundo as características dos itens que representam.

1. kinds of nouns* **proper:** Mary, Japan, July **common:** boy, dog, day **concrete:** bread, coffee, oil **abstract:** love, beauty, pain **collective:** band, crowd, flock **countable:** book, bus, egg **uncountable:** water, salt, food	**3. number** **singular:** box, cup, glass **plural:** boxes, cups, glasses [ver Plural of Nouns, p. 129]
2. gender **masculine:** man, king, lion **feminine:** girl, queen, lioness **common:** child, student, teacher **neuter:** chair, tree, school [ver Gender of Nouns, p. 71]	**4. function** **subject: Maria** is intelligent. **object:** They invited **the pilot**. I spoke to **the boy**. **complement:** He is **my father**. **agent:** It was built by **the girls**. etc.

* As classificações podem variar; ver Abstract Nouns, p. 09; Collective Nouns, p. 41; Countable & Uncountable Nouns, p. 51.

Exercises [answers on p. 200]

1 Classify the underlined nouns as C (concrete) or A (abstract).

1. Gold, <u>silver</u> and iron are substances.   _C_
2. I can't stand the <u>injustices</u> of men.   ____
3. Money can't buy <u>happiness</u>.   ____
4. I have no <u>idea</u> where the dog is.   ____
5. A temple is a place of <u>silence</u>.   ____
6. My <u>house</u> is north of the lake.   ____

2 **Underline the uncountable nouns.**
1. I like eggs and milk in the morning.
2. We haven't got much rice.
3. My ring is made of gold.
4. Love rules the life of many women.
5. The bread Grandma prepares is delicious.
6. You can drink some fresh water.

3 **Match the pairs according to their gender.**
1. husband   __2__ a. niece
2. nephew   _____ b. mother-in-law
3. son   _____ c. princess
4. uncle   _____ d. daughter
5. father-in-law   _____ e. wife
6. prince   _____ f. aunt

4 **Underline the correct alternative.**
1. Those (woman, women) are working hard.
2. Is the (child, children) home?
3. The (baby, babies) are sleeping now.
4. How many (knife, knives) are there?
5. Your new hat is in that (box, boxes).
6. The (peach, peaches) are delicious.

5 **Classify the underlined words as S (subject) or O (object).**
1. My bother painted his bike.   __O__
2. My friends skate every morning.   _____
3. Alice, Carol and Jane are sisters.   _____
4. The girls looked at the actor and smiled.   _____
5. Did the teacher talk to your father?   _____
6. The kids had dinner and went to bed.   _____

48 Nouns II

Form

Em inglês, para criar novos substantivos é comum:

1. a junção de palavras:	3. o uso do gerúndio e do infinitivo:
blackboard **note**book **father**-in-law **swimming**-pool	He lives in the red **building**. **Running** is my pastime. **To study** Math is difficult for me.
2. o uso da mesma palavra em funções diferentes:	4. o uso de prefixos ou sufixos:
He is **poor** and sick. (adj.) Give money to the **poor**. (subst.) **Address** me the letter. (v.) What's your **address**? (subst.)	dance → danc**er** happy → happin**ess** difficult → difficult**y**

Sufixos e prefixos adicionados a verbos, adjetivos ou outros substantivos criam um enorme número de novos substantivos.

Principais sufixos	Principais prefixos
-acy/-cy: priv**acy** **-age:** cour**age** **-an:** librari**an** **-ance:** assist**ance** **-tion/-ion:** ac**tion** **-dom:** king**dom** **-er/-or:** read**er**, act**or** **-hood:** child**hood** **-ism:** social**ism** **-ist:** geolog**ist** **-ity/-ty:** char**ity** **-ment:** treat**ment** **-ness:** kind**ness** **-ship:** friend**ship** **-y:** societ**y**	**a-:** **a**theist **anti-:** **anti**septic **arch-:** **arch**duke **auto-:** **auto**graph **bi-:** **bi**plane **dis-:** **dis**belief **inter-:** **inter**cept **mis-:** **mis**belief **non-:** **non**sense **out-:** **out**come **re-:** **re**action **sub-:** **sub**way **sur-:** **sur**name **trans-:** **trans**cript etc.

Exercises [answers on p. 201]

1 Match the columns and build compound nouns.

1. life
2. gold
3. grand
4. teen
5. camp
6. tooth
7. door
8. house

a. fish: _____
b. fire: _____
c. keeper: _____
d. bell: _____
e. ager: _____
f. time: *lifetime*
g. paste: _____
h. mother: _____

2 Underline the verbs that can function as nouns. Then choose one to complete the sentence.

1. access – beauty – comb   That was not the ___*access*___ to the beach.
2. box – dream – daisy   She didn't remember her night _____ .
3. answer – face – orange   I looked at her _____ and smiled.
4. day – milk – name   What's his _____ ?
5. question – now – step   He asked me a _____ .
6. late – hope – kiss   I gave him a _____ and left.
7. race – paint – only   Is the going to win the _____ ?
8. walk – wolf – show   Let's go out for a _____ ?

3 Add a suffix to the word given and complete the sentence.

-er -ing -ion -ism -ment -ness -ship -y

1. (build) My family lives in that red ___*building*___ .
2. (win) She wants to be the _____ at the contest.
3. (except) The _____ provides the rule.
4. (quiet) _____ is a great treasure.
5. (friend) You are responsible for a broken _____ .
6. (social) He believes _____ can save the world.
7. (treat) There is no cure without the correct _____ .
8. (honest) _____ is the best policy.

49 Numerals

Cardinal and ordinal numbers – list

Cardinal Numbers							
1	one	13	thirteen	25	twenty-five
2	two	14	fourteen	26	twenty-six
3	three	15	fifteen	27	twenty-seven
4	four	16	sixteen	28	twenty-eight
5	five	17	seventeen	29	twenty-nine
6	six	18	eighteen	30	thirty
7	seven	19	nineteen	40	forty
8	eight	20	twenty	50	fifty
9	nine	21	twenty-one	60	sixty
10	ten	22	twenty-two	70	seventy
11	eleven	23	twenty-three	80	eighty
12	twelve	24	twenty-four	90	ninety

100	one/a hundred	1,000,000	one/a million
1,000	one/a thousand	1,000,100	one/a million and a hundred

How to Read

Thousands – 15,560: fifteen thousand five hundred (and) sixty.
Millions – 2,450,000: two million four hundred (and) fifty thousand.
Decimals – 2.36: two point three six.
Percentages – 37%: thirty seven percent.
Fractions – ⅜: three eighths; **¼:** one quarter; **⅔:** two thirds; **½:** one half.

Dates

1500: fifteen hundred **or** one thousand five hundred.
1999: nineteen ninety-nine **or** nineteen hundred (and) ninety-nine **or** one thousand nine hundred (and) ninety-nine.

2000: two thousand **or** twenty hundred **or** two triple-oh.
2001: two thousand (and) one **or** twenty hundred (and) one **or** twenty oh-one.
2010: two thousand (and) ten **or** twenty hundred (and) ten **or** twenty ten **or** two-oh-one-oh.

Ordinal Numbers			
1st	first	21th	twenty-first
2nd	second	22nd	twenty- second
3rd	third	23rd	twenty-third
4th	fourth	24th	twenty-fourth
5th	fifth	25th	twenty-fifth
6th	sixth	26th	twenty-sixth
7th	seventh	27th	twenty-seventh
8th	eighth	28th	twenty-eighth
9th	ninth	29th	twenty-ninth
10th	tenth	30th	thirtieth
11th	eleventh	40th	fortieth
12th	twelfth	50th	fiftieth
13th	thirteenth	60th	sixtieth
14th	fourteenth	70th	seventieth
15th	fifteenth	80th	eightieth
16th	sixteenth	90th	ninetieth
17th	seventeenth	100th	one hundredth
18th	eighteenth	1,000th	one thousandth
19th	nineteenth	1,000,000th	one millionth
20th	twentieth	1,000,100th	one million and a hundredth

Notes – Em números compostos apenas o último é ordinal.
632nd : six hundred and thirty-second. **4,110th :** four thousand one hundred and tenth.

Titles

No inglês oral, fala-se o artigo **the** antes do número ordinal.

Charles II: Charles the Second.
Edward VI: Edward the Sixth.
Henry VIII: Henry the Eighth.

50 One

One pode funcionar como adjetivo, substantivo ou pronome e expressar coisas diversas.

One or two people hate him.
They had lunch at **one**.
One can see the city from here.

1. One/s (um/a)	**2. One** (se, a pessoa)
quantidade, particularização:	quem fala ou ouve; nem sempre é traduzido:
I want **one** bar of chocolate.	**One** must follow the principles **one** believes.
One of the cats is here.	(É preciso seguir os princípios nos quais se acredita.)
I talked to **one** Mr. Brown.	
I hate this pen, give me that **one**.	

Form
one/s (um/ns, uma/s): **One** of the doctors is absent.
one's (seu/s, sua/s): People have to respect **one's** ideas.
oneself (si mesmo/a): One must respect **oneself**.

Agreement
one: verbo no singular
If **one** fails, **one has** to try harder next time.
ones: verbo no plural
Try those cakes. The **ones** with cream **are** delicious.

Exercises [answers on p. 201]

1 Underline the correct verb form.
1. More than one boy (is, are) late.
2. One out of four students (gets, get) this question wrong.
3. The best ones (is, are) going to receive a medal.
4. One's experiences (is, are) more important than advices.

5. (Is, Are) these the ones you want?
6. One (has, have) to learn from one's mistakes.
7. One book (was, were) taken.
8. One of the questions (is, are) wrong.

② Write one in the correct place.
1. I'm just _____ one _____ player on the _____ team.
2. That is the _____ person she wanted to marry _____ .
3. She's the _____ I like the best _____ .
4. There is _____ only _____ left.
5. _____ Babies start to talk at _____ .
6. Have you _____ got _____ ?
7. _____ John Doe made a speech _____ .
8. Problems should come _____ at a _____ time!
9. _____ can catch fine trout in this _____ river.
10. You _____ will see him _____ day.

③ Check the best translation.
1. One should ask oneself what the correct attitude is.
   a. É preciso se perguntar qual a atitude correta. ✓
   b. Você deve perguntar a alguém qual sua atitude correta.
2. One shouldn't ask that question.
   a. Você não deve fazer aquela pergunta.
   b. Não se deve fazer tal pergunta.
3. You must follow the principles you believe.
   a. Deve-se seguir os princípios nos quais se acredita.
   b. Você deve seguir seus princípios e crer neles.
4. One should always wash one's hands.
   a. Deve-se lavar as mãos sempre.
   b. Lave suas mãos sempre.
5. One must be conscientious about one's hygiene.
   a. É preciso conscientizar-se sobre questões de higiene.
   b. Deve-se ter consciência sobre a própria higiene.

51 Ordinary Verbs

Em inglês a maioria dos verbos é comum (main verb/ordinary/common):

come   give   go   know   look   make   think   try   want   work
etc.

1. Main Verb é o verbo principal da frase. Pode estar sozinho ou junto a um verbo auxiliar. I **work**. I am **working**. I can **work**. Does he **work**?	**3. Present Simple** A 3ª pess. do sing. recebe -s/-es. He talk**s**. She teach**es**. He run**s**.
2. Main Parts base: talk go present simple: talk/s go/es past simple: talked went past participle: talked gone present participle: talking going	**4. Past Simple, Past Participle** podem ser: regulares: verbo + -d/-ed They work**ed** hard. irregulares: não seguem normas They **went** home. [ver p. 217 Irregular Verbs]
5. o auxiliar do (do /does/ did) forma a negativa e a interrogativa do presente e passado. affirmative: I go. He goes. He went. negative: I **do not** go. He **does not** go. He **did not** go. interrogative: **Do** I go? **Does** he go? **Did** he go?	

Note – o verbo principal permanece na forma base quando acompanhado pelo auxiliar Do: He doesn't work; Did he arrive?

Exercises [answers on p. 202]

Underline the main verbs in the following sentences.

1. Michael <u>was</u> a good singer.
2. They are waiting for you in the lab.

3. She has two brothers and a sister.
4. I have lived in Japan.
5. Ann does the housework every day.
6. I don't do the dishes after lunch.
7. Karl doesn't speak Italian.
8. I always swim at the club.
9. My parents had a house by the lake.
10. They didn't have a boat.

Underline the correct alternative.

1. My brother always (<u>chooses</u>, choose) the wrong answer.
2. The kids (likes, like) science fiction.
3. Jane (lives, live) in Rio.
4. I (talk, talked) to them last week.
5. Linda and Alex (speaks, speak) Italian.
6. They (walked, walk) home last night.
7. I (wrote, write) a love letter yesterday.
8. They (likes, liked) the show last week.
9. She (understands, understand) what I say.
10. The boys (wants, wanted) to go to the club.

Check the correct interrogative or negative form for the sentences below.

1. We went to work by car.
   a. We didn't go to work by car. ✓
   b. We didn't went to work by car.
2. She washes the car on Sundays.
   a. Does she wash the car on Sundays?
   b. Do she washes the car on Sundays?
3. I know what to do.
   a. I know what to don't.
   b. I don't know what to do.
4. They arrived early yesterday.
   a. Did they arrive early yesterday?
   b. They didn't arrived early yesterday.
5. I study in the evening.
   a. I didn't study in the evening.
   b. Do you study in the evening?

52 Participles

Present & Past

Um **particípio** é uma forma verbal. Em inglês temos: o Particípio Presente (verbo + **-ing**[1]) e o Particípio Passado (verbo + **-ed** ou verbo irregular).

amaz**ing**   interest**ing**   amaz**ed**   interest**ed**   tak**en**

São usados:

como adjetivo: That was an **amazing** evening. He is **interested** in Literature. **em progressive e perfect tenses e passive voice:** I am **writing**. I have **worked** hard. He was **taken** to hospital.	**depois de verbos de percepção[2]:** I heard the baby **crying**. I smelled the cake **burning**. **para encurtar/juntar frases:** I saw the dog. It slept on the sofa. I saw the dog **sleeping** on the sofa.

Note – (1) o Gerúndio, também formado por verbo + **-ing**, é usado como substantivo.
(2) verbos de percepção: see, watch, hear, listen, smell, feel etc.

Exercises [answers on p. 202]

1 Circle Pr (present) or Pt (past) to classify the underlined participle.

1. The crying baby had a wet diaper.   (Pr)   Pt
2. The boys ran away in a stolen car.   Pr   Pt
3. I walked away from the laughing girls.   Pr   Pt
4. We saw the car coming around the corner.   Pr   Pt
5. I heard my friend talking on the phone.   Pr   Pt
6. The worried doctors went to a private room.   Pr   Pt
7. The confused ladies didn't know where to go.   Pr   Pt
8. Going to Japan they expected better jobs.   Pr   Pt
9. I felt the house shaking.   Pr   Pt
10. I feel frightened after watching a horror film.   Pr   Pt

2 Choose the correct participle to complete the sentence.

1. The kids were (frightening, <u>frightened</u>) because they had seen a rat.
2. She said that babysitting was an (exhausting, exhausted) task.
3. I get (boring, bored) when I go to formal events.
4. Today, the news on TV were (depressing, depressed).
5. I got (depressing, depressed) after watching the news.
6. Your kid was (fascinating, fascinated) by the book I gave him.
7. The concert was (exciting, excited).
8. This is an (interesting, interested) story.
9. He feels (frustrating, frustrated) when he can't express himself well.

3 Complete the sentences with words from the box.

| ~~broken~~ | running | repaired | talking | disappointed |
| wrecked | bored | tired | shocking | |

1. He has to fix a _____ *broken* _____ computer.
2. The _____ students kept suddenly quiet.
3. The singer talked to the _____ fans.
4. The _____ water was clean and fresh.
5. He walked away from the _____ car.
6. She never got back her _____ watch.
7. The audience was really _____ by the long speech.
8. I feel so _____ that I'm going to take a rest.
9. The man's language was _____.

4 Write the present and past participle of the following verbs.

1. give: *giving, given*   take: _____
2. write: _____   speak: _____
3. do: _____   fall: _____

53 Passive Voice

A **voz passiva** é formada por **to be**[1] + **verbo no particípio passado**.

É usada quando o agente da ação não é conhecido ou não se deseja enfatizá-lo. Quando mencionado, fica no final da frase depois da preposição **by**.

active voice　　　　　　**passive voice**[2]
He **sang** a song.　→　A song **was sung** by him.
I **fix** cars.　　　→　Cars **are fixed** by me.

Active voice →		Passive voice
present simple:	drive/s	**is/are** driven
past simple:	drove	**was/were** driven
future simple:	will drive;	**will be** driven
	is/are going to drive	**is/are going to** be driven
present progressive:	is/are driving	**is/are being** driven
past progressive:	was/were driving	**was/were being** driven
present perfect:	has/have driven	**has/have been** driven
past perfect:	had driven	**had been** driven
conditional:	would drive	**would be** driven
modals:	can/could drive etc.	**can/could be** driven etc.

Notes – **(1)** na passiva, **to be** assume o tempo do verbo da voz ativa; **(2)** Se na voz ativa o verbo tem **dois objetos**, qualquer deles pode ser sujeito da passiva: I gave him a book → A book was given to him./He was given a book (by me).

Exercises [answers on p. 203]

1 Complete the sentences in the passive voice. Use the correct verb form.

Active Voice　　　　　　　　　　Passive Voice
1. You can take the book.　　　　The book ___*can be taken*___ by you.
2. They must obey the rules.　　　The rules _____ by them.
3. The kids broke the window.　　The window _____ .

4. We will give a party here. A party _____ here.
5. They ate some rice. Some rice _____ by them.
6. I was cleaning the house. The house _____ .
7. He wrote the letters yesterday. The letters _____ yesterday.
8. He pays us on Mondays. We _____ on Mondays.

2 Rewrite the sentences in the passive voice.

1. Jean pays the employees at the end of the week.
   The employees are paid _____ at the end of the week.
2. The Owens have sold the old brick house.
   _____ by the Owens.
3. Mike had bought your old bike when I arrived.
   _____ by Mike when I arrived.
4. We would cook dinner if we could.
   _____ by us if we could.
5. The girls are painting the gate near the old house.
   _____ by girls.
6. They have canceled the show because of the rain.
   _____ because of the rain.
7. We are going to repair the car after the game.
   The car _____ by us after the game.
8. She has dropped some tea on the carpet.
   _____ on the carpet.

3 Rewrite the two possible passive sentences.

1. I will give her a gold ring. *She wil be given a gold ring,*
   A gold ring will be given to her.
2. They told us the truth.
3. He showed Ann his new cars.
4. We have taught French to Paul.
5. I offered Ted a job.
6. Fran has sent me a letter.

54 Past Tenses I

General table

Vários tempos verbais podem expressar ações passadas ou que têm alguma relação com o passado.

verb tense	expresses
past simple verbo (+d/ed) verbo irregular	ação terminada em tempo definido: My class **finished** at ten yesterday. The train **left** at six last week.
past progressive was/were + v.-ing	ação em andamento no passado: I **was working** when you called. We **were studying** while he **was sleeping**.
past perfect had + v. pp[1]	ação realizada antes de outra ação no passado: We **had cooked** lunch before you arrived. I **had left** home before he called.
past perfect progressive had been + v.-ing	ênfase na duração da ação: He **had been working** for hours before dinner. I **had been reading** before I went to bed.
present perfect[2] have/has + v. pp	ação iniciada no passado e ainda acontecendo; ação recentemente terminada: I **have waited** for 2 hours.[3] She **has** just **left**.
present perfect progressive[2] have/has been + v.-ing	ênfase na duração da ação: I **have been waiting** for hours. She **has been washing** the garden all day.

Notes – **(1) Abreviations: v.** = verbo; **pp =** past participle. **(2)** o **Present Perfect** e o **Present Perfect Progressive** são tempos que podem fazer referência ao presente e ao passado. **(3) Tradução:** Espero há duas horas; Ela acaba de sair.

Exercises [answers on p. 204]

1 **Identify the types of action.**

a. finished action at a definite past time
b. ongoing action in the past
c. past action anterior to another past action
d. focus in the action

1. The sun rose at 5:30 this morning. _____a_____
2. The train had departed when he arrived at the station. _____
3. What time did the meeting begin? _____
4. The students were writing the composition when Frank fainted. _____
5. I was singing while she played the guitar. _____
6. I had cleaned the kitchen when she arrived. _____
7. We had been painting the fence all day long. _____
8. Shakespeare wrote *Othello* in 1603. _____

2 **Check the correct alternative.**

1. While I _____ the film there was a power-cut.
   a. have watched   b. was watching ✓   c. had watched
2. She _____ to that dentist before so she trusted him.
   a. had been   b. was going   c. went
3. I _____ to the lawyer when I saw your sister.
   a. talked   b. was talking   c. have talked
4. While he _____ her bike she arrived.
   a. was repairing   b. had repaired   c. repaired
5. I didn't know you _____ a new house.
   a. were buying   b. bought   c. had bought
6. What _____ to the wedding yesterday?
   a. did you wear   b. were you wearing   c. had you worn
7. When I woke up I remembered what _____ .
   a. had happened   b. was happening   c. happened
8. Who _____ the car at the time of the accident?
   a. had driven   b. was driving   c. drove

55 Past Tenses II

Past progressive

O *past progressive* expressa ações em andamento no passado.

The sun **was shining** at 5:30.   He **was sleeping** at 8:00.

É usado em conjunto com o *past simple* e com palavras como: *yesterday, ... ago, in June, at..., when, while* etc.

While I **was jogging** the dog bit me.   They **were working** when I arrived.

Past Progressive (be + v.-ing)	
to walk – affirmative	
I **was**	We **were**
You **were** walking	You **were** walking
He/She/It **was**	They **were**

Forms	
interrogative:	question:
Was he walking?	**Where** was he walking?
negative:	short answer:
He was **not** walking.	Yes, he **was**.
negative-interrogative:	No, he **wasn't**.
Wasn't he walking?	contracted form:
	was not: **wasn't**
	were not: **weren't**

Spelling

Ao receber **-ing** a maioria dos verbos não sofre alteração:

do – doing   buy – buying   porém, verbo em:

1. e:	2. ie:	3. c.v.c¹ (sílaba tônica):
perde o e	muda para y	dobra a consoante
ride – riding	die – dying	run – running
write – writing	lie – lying	begin – beginning
		occur – occurring

Note – (1) c/v/c: consoante/ vogal/ consoante

Exercises [answers on p. 204]

1 Complete the sentences with the past progressive of the given verbs.

1. (sleep) We _____ *were sleeping* _____ when the phone rang.
2. (ride) Tom _____ his bike when he saw you.
3. (cut) Sheila _____ bread when she cut herself.
4. (study, swim) While I _____ they _____ .
5. (drive) At 4:00 this afternoon, Bob _____ his new car.
6. (lie) When she talked to me I knew she _____ .
7. (play) They _____ tennis when the accident happened.
8. (win) When I left the club my team _____ .

2 Match questions and answers.

a. Yes, they were.
b. No, he wasn't.
c. At home.
d. To the lawyer.
e. Yes, I was
f. Because he was tired.
g. I was doing an exercise.
h. They were watching TV.

1. Where was he studying? ___c___
2. What were you doing an hour ago? _____
3. Was he working when the house shook? _____
4. Who were they talking to when I left the room? _____
5. Were the children playing when you left home? _____
6. What were they doing while I was sleeping? _____
7. Why was the baby crying? _____
8. Were you late for class yesterday? _____

56 Past Tenses III

Past simple – regular verbs

O **passado simples** é usado para expressar ações ocorridas no passado. É usado com palavras como: *yesterday, last..., ...ago, in...* etc.

O verbo regular tem a terminação **-ed/-d**.

I **talked** to her one hour ago.   He **studied** hard when he was a child.

Past Simple (verbo regular) to work – affirmative			
I You He, She, It	worked	We You They	worked

Forms	
interrogative: Did he work?	question: Where did he work?
negative: He did not work.	short answer: Yes, he did. No, he didn't.
negative-interrogative: Didn't he work?	contracted form: did not: didn't

Note – quando usado com o auxiliar **did**, o verbo principal fica no infinitivo **sem to**.

Spelling

A maioria dos verbos apenas recebe **-ed:**

play – play**ed**   talk – talk**ed**   mas, verbo terminado em:

1. e:	2. consoante + y:	3. c.v.c (sílaba tônica):
recebe -d	o y muda para i	dobra a consoante
like - like**d**	carry - carr**ied**	stop - sto**pp**ed
live - live**d**	study - stud**ied**	occur - occu**rr**ed
		permit - permi**tt**ed

Exercises [answers on p. 204]

1 Write the past form of the verbs below.

1. like — *liked*
2. care —
3. admit —
4. hurry —
5. talk —
6. prefer —
7. enjoy —
8. plan —
9. study —
10. rob —

2 Rewrite the sentences according to the information given.

1. (int.) He arrived late last night. — *Did he arrive late last night?*
2. (neg.) We played golf yesterday. —
3. (neg.) She loved him years ago. —
4. (int.) You talked to the teacher. —
5. (What) Paul studied math. —
6. (Where) I hurried to school. —

3 Complete the sentences with the past simple of the verbs given.

1. (rain) It _____ *rained* _____ hard last night.
2. (stop) He _____ writing when I entered the room.
3. (dance) We _____ for hours last night.
4. (watch) The children _____ TV in the afternoon.
5. (study) I _____ Italian when I lived in Italy.
6. (bake) Did Mom _____ a cake for your birthday?
7. (cook) You didn't _____ dinner yesterday.
8. (arrive) What time did they _____?

57 Past Tenses IV

Past simple – irregular verbs

Verbos irregulares não seguem normas fixas para formação do passado:
[ver Lista p. 217]

    sleep – slept   go – went   think – thought   etc.

Past Simple (verbo irregular)

to sleep – affirmative

I		We	
You	slept	You	slept
He, She, It		They	

Forms

interrogative:
Did he sleep?

negative:
He did **not** sleep.

negative-interrogative:
Didn't he sleep?

question:
Where did he sleep?

short answer:
Yes, he **did**.
No, he **didn't**.

contracted form:
did not: **didn't**

Notes – **interrogative**: auxiliar antes do sujeito; **question**: palavra interrogativa antes do auxiliar; **negative**: auxiliar + not; **negative-interrogative**: auxiliar negativo e contraído antes do sujeito; o **verbo principal** fica no infinitivo sem **to** quando usado com o auxiliar did.

Exercises [answers on p. 205]

1 Write the past form of the verbs below.

1. take   *took*
2. make
3. do
4. be

P | 121

5. have _____
6. come _____
7. put _____
8. read _____
9. teach _____
10. buy _____

2 Rewrite the sentences according to the information given.

1. (int.) He came home late. *Did he come home late?*
2. (neg.) We swam yesterday. _____
3. (neg.) She left him years ago. _____
4. (What) Paul bought a tie. _____
5. (Where) I went to the Zoo on Sunday. _____

3 Check the correct alternative.

1. Mr. Johnson _____ the room a few minutes ago.
   a. leave   b. didn't live   c. left ✓
2. Your brother _____ me on the head last class.
   a. hit   b. didn't hitted   c. hot
3. I _____ my books. Did you _____ yours?
   a. bring; brought b. brought; brought   c. brought; bring
4. My sister _____ her car keys.
   a. lived   b. lost   c. didn't left
5. He _____ up smoking some years ago.
   a. given   b. not give   c. gave
6. I didn't _____ the last question.
   a. understand   b. understood   c. understand not
7. Did your parents _____ to the seaside last summer?
   a. didn't go   b. went   c. go
8. We _____ them some games yesterday.
   a. taught   b. thought   c. fought

4 Answer the questions about yourself.

1. Where did you go yesterday? _____.
2. Who did you see yesterday? _____.
3. What time did you leave home? _____.
4. What time did you go back home? _____.

58 Past Tenses V

Past perfect & past perfect progressive

O *past perfect* indica a ação que ocorreu antes de outra no passado. O *past perfect progressive* enfatiza tal ação.

I **had eaten** a sandwich when they arrived.
I **had been eating** for hours when they arrived.

São geralmente usados com palavras como: *when, before, after* etc.

He called you after I **had left**.[1]
I **had been cleaning** the room before she came home.

Past Perfect	Past Perfect Progressive
had + v. pp[2]	had been + v.-ing
to eat – affirmative	**to eat – affirmative**
I	I
You	You
He, She, It had eaten.	He, She, It had been eating.
We	We
You	You
They	They

Forms	
interrogative:	question:
Had he eaten?	**What** had he eaten?
Had he been eating?	**What** had he been eating?
negative:	short answer:
He had **not** eaten.	Yes, he **had**.
He had **not** been eating.	No, he **hadn't**.
negative-interrogative:	contracted form:
Hadn't he eaten?	had: **'d**
Hadn't he been eating?	had not : **hadn't**

Notes – **(1) tradução:** Ele te ligou após eu ter saído; Eu tinha estado limpando a sala antes dela voltar para casa. **(2) v.:** verbo; **pp:** past participle.

Exercises [answers on p. 205]

1 **Rewrite the sentences using the information given.**

1. I had read his books before he became famous.
   (int.) _____*Had you read his book*_____ before he became famous?
2. The plane had landed by the time we got to the airport.
   (neg.) _____ by the time we got to the airport?
3. They had been to Asia many times before.
   (Where) _____ many times before?
4. Paul had been waiting for Carol for hours.
   (Who) _____ for hours?
5. She had played our song before we arrived.
   (What) _____ before we arrived?

2 **Complete the sentences with the past perfect of the verbs given.**

1. (leave) I _____*had left*_____ the room before the bell rang.
2. (finish) When we arrived, they _____ the meeting.
3. (give) We left after we _____ the flowers to her.
4. (have) They were happy because they _____ good grades.
5. (do) He played video games after he _____ his homework.
6. (destroy) When Mom arrived, the dog _____ the garden.
7. (live) He told me that he _____ in Greece.
8. (miss) She was late because she _____ the bus.

3 **Underline the correct alternative.**

1. He said that we (<u>had hurt</u>; being hurt) him.
2. I admired him for what he (had been doing; had did).
3. By the time we arrived there, everybody (left; had left).
4. I knew she (didn't win; hadn't won) the championship the year before.
5. He (was; had been) a sailor before he started teaching.
6. I (had said; said) that I had been to the pyramids before.
7. After we had seen the lions, we (had left, left) the Zoo.
8. They (had been working; hadn't work) hard.

59 Personal Pronouns

Subject & object

Subject		Object	
I	(eu)	me	(me, mim; comigo)
you	(tu, você)	you	(te, ti; contigo)
he	(ele)	him	(o, lhe, se, si; consigo)
she	(ela)	her	(a, lhe, se, si; consigo)
it	(ele/ela)	it	(o,a, lhe, se, si; consigo)
we	(nós)	us	(nos; conosco)
you	(vós, vocês)	you	(vos; convosco)
they	(eles, elas)	them	(os, as, se,si, lhes; consigo)

Pronomes pessoais substituem substantivos. Podem funcionar como sujeito ou objeto.

Subject	Object
They love the kids.	The teacher loves **them**.
We are friends.	Mary talked to **him**.
She speaks English.	He bought **it**.

Alguns verbos podem ter dois objetos, **(1)** direto e **(2)** indireto:

   She gave the book to me.
      (1) (2)

   She told us a story.
    (2) (1)

Exercises [answers on p. 206]

1 Classify the underlined pronouns as: S (for subject) or O (for object).

		S	O
1.	He is my brother and I respect him.		O
2.	They are my parents and they travel a lot.		
3.	We are brother and sister.		
4.	She is my teacher. Her name is Julie.		
5.	I know that you don't like me.		
6.	He was glad to get the new ID.		
7.	Are they going to follow us?		
8.	I am going to see him today.		
9.	If you find my cell phone, give it to me, please.		
10.	The boys were late. They missed the show.		

2 Underline the correct pronoun.

1. I think (I – Me) am in trouble.
2. (They – Them) named their daughter Francesca.
3. Our friends love (us – we).
4. He was disappointed to see (she – her) at the club.
5. They can't see (you – she).
6. You can talk to (they – me).
7. She looked at (they – them) and went home.
8. The doctor will see (he – him) in five minutes.
9. That depends on (me – she).
10. Pass (I – me) the sugar, please!

3 Substitute the underlined words. Use pronouns.

1. We ate fish for dinner.   _it_
2. Snow and ice covered the roads.   _____
3. The children are playing with a dog.   _____
4. Doctor Jim Brown has arrived.   _____
5. You can talk to the doctor.   _____
6. Daniel has invited Josh and me to the party.   _____
7. We have to wash the dogs today.   _____
8. I admire our teachers.   _____
9. Where is Sally? The girls want to go out with Sally.   _____

60 Phrasal Verb List

Phrasal verb é um verbo que muda de significado ao receber o acréscimo de uma partícula (preposição ou advérbio). O *phrasal verb* pode ser *separable* (verbo e partícula podem ser separados pelo objeto) ou *inseparable* (verbo e partícula não podem ser separados).

I **called** Mary **up**.　　　　　　　He **called off** the concert.

ask out: convidar para sair	Why did you **ask** her **out**?
bring about: causar	The economic crisis **brought about** changes in people's habits.
bring up: criar alguém ou algo	I **brought** my sisters **up**.
burn down: destruir com fogo	The house **burnt down** in 2 hours.
call back: retornar um telefonema	I'll **call** you **back** in some minutes.
call in: convidar formalmente	He **called** all the editors **in** for a talk.
call off: cancelar	They **called off** the flight because of the weather conditions.
call on:* visitar	I **called on** Sam last week.
call up: telefonar	He **called** me **up** to talk about you.
catch up:* alcançar o mesmo nível	Work hard to **catch up** to the other students.
check in:* registrar-se	**Check in** two hours before your flight.
check out:* sair	We have to **check out** before 2:00 p.m.
come across:* encontrar por acaso	I **came across** my old ID yesterday.
cross out: eliminar	**Cross** the incorrect words **out**.
cut out: parar de	They'll **cut out** working on Fridays.
do over: redecorar	I'll **do over** the bedroom.
drop by*/**in:*** visitar sem avisar	He said he'll **drop by** some day.
drop off: deixar	He **dropped** me **off** near my house.
drop out:* abandonar	She **dropped out** of school in May.
figure out: entender	I can't **figure out** this math problem.
fill in/out: completar formulário	**Fill in** the form before the interview.
get along:* ter bom relacionamento	I **get along** with my step-mother.
get off:* sair de ônibus, trem, avião	**Get off** the bus near the park.
get on:* entrar em ônibus, trem, avião	He **got on** the wrong bus.

* inseparable

get over:* recuperar-se	Did Grandma **get over** the flu?
get through:* terminar, sobreviver	He **got through** all the tasks and left.
get up:* levantar	Do you **get up** at six on Sundays?
give up: parar de	I **gave up** smoking a year ago.
go over:* rever	**Go over** this work and correct any possible mistakes!
hand in: entregar	**Hand in** the form before Friday.
hang up: desligar o telefone	Wait a minute. Don't **hang up**.
keep up with:* ficar no mesmo nível	It's difficult to **keep up** with Paul.
look after:* cuidar	I **looked after** her baby for a couple of hours.
look down on: considerar como inferior	He **looks down** on anyone who is not from his country.
look for: tentar achar	She **looked for** a red pair of shoes.
look into:* investigar	Can you **look into** this matter for me, please?
look up: procurar por	**Look** this word **up** in the dictionary.
make up: inventar	Mom **makes up** nice animal stories.
pass away:* morrer	Grandpa **passed away** peacefully.
pass out: desmaiar*; distribuir	I **passed out** when I heard about the accident.
pick up: dar carona	Can you **pick** me **up** at five?
put away: pôr em local apropriado	Please, **put away** the icecream before it melts.
put off: adiar	I **put off** the show because of the weather conditions.
put out: extinguir	The firemen **put out** the fire.
put up with:* tolerar	I can't **put up with** all this noise.
run into:* encontrar por acaso	We **ran into** Dad downtown!
run out of:* terminar, ficar sem	We've **ran out of** sugar!
show up:* aparecer	I had invited Tom but he didn't **show up**.
shut off: parar algo	You have to **shut off** the machine at the end of the week.
take after:* parecer-se	Does he **take after** his mother?
take out: sair com alguém	He **took** us **out** for dinner.
take over: ter o controle	She **took over** all the investigation.
think over: considerar	I'll **think over** her proposal carefully.
throw up: vomitar	I nearly threw up when I saw the rotten fish.
try on: testar, experimentar	May I **try** it **on**? I'm not sure about the size.
turn off: desligar	**Turn** it **off**, please. It's too nosy!

* inseparable

61 Plural of Nouns

Regular Plural

O **plural** da maioria dos substantivos é expresso por meio do sufixo **-s**.

girl**s** book**s** zebra**s** tree**s** house**s** roof**s** proof**s** day**s** etc.

Porém, dependendo da terminação, algumas palavras sofrem alterações.

1. palavras em **o, s, ss, sh, ch, x, z** + **-es**	3. doze palavras em **f/fe**
heroes boxes quizzes peaches misses bushes buses	f/fe mudam para v + -es calf – cal**ves** sheaf – shea**ves** knife – kni**ves** shelf – shel**ves** leaf – lea**ves** thief – thie**ves** life – li**ves** wolf – wol**ves** loaf – loa**ves** half – hal**ves** self – sel**ves** wife – wi**ves**
2. palavras em **consoante + y** y muda para i + -es: city – cit**ies** lilly – lil**ies** lady – lad**ies** hobby – hobb**ies**	

Irregular Plural

Algumas palavras fazem o plural de forma irregular:

child – children   man – men   woman – women
foot – feet   mouse – mice   deer – deer
goose – geese   tooth – teeth   sheep – sheep

Notes – (a) recebem -s: pianos, photos, radios, videos, kilos **(b) estão sempre no plural:** scissors, pants, glasses, pyjamas etc. **(c) compound nouns:** geralmente pluraliza-se a última palavra – bus stops, drive-ins, cupfuls

Exercises [answers on p. 206]

1 Rewrite the words in the plural form.

1. bush _bushes_
2. cherry _____
3. cliff _____
4. boss _____
5. beauty _____
6. self _____

7. goose _____
8. family _____
9. donkey _____
10. child _____
11. chimney _____
12. echo _____
13. foot _____
14. diary _____

2 Underline the correct alternative.

1. My (<u>baby</u>; babies) is crying.
2. Take those (dress; dresses) to your room.
3. Do you like (strawberry; strawberries)?
4. There are some (mouse, mice) in the basement.
5. Go wash your (feet; foot). They are dirty!
6. We have eaten two (sandwich; sandwiches) each.
7. I want two (spoonfuls, spoonfulies) of sugar, please.
8. His (trouser; trousers) were new and expensive.

3 Check the correct sentences. Correct the mistakes.

1. I have two brothers and three sisters.   ✓
2. I found two boxes of potatoes on the beach.   _____
3. We offered them some glass of fresh water.   _____
4. The foxes ran after the old ladies.   _____
5. The handkerchiefs are on the first shelf.   _____
6. Make 3 wishs before cutting the cake.   _____
7. There were many flys on the peaches.   _____
8. Those are the men who sell sheep.   _____

4 Rewrite the sentences in the plural form.

1. This old watch is lovely.
   These <u>old watches are lovely.</u>
2. There is an old church around the park.
   There are _____
3. I am sure he is a good child.
   We are sure _____
4. Did the policeman arrest the thief?
   Did the _____
5. Is there any knife in the drawer?
   Are there any _____
6. He is going to tell me an interesting story.
   They are going to tell us _____

62 Possessive Adjectives & Pronouns

possessive adjectives		possessive pronouns	
my	(meu, minha)	mine	(o meu, a minha)
your	(teu, tua)	yours	(o teu, a tua)
his	(dele)	his	(o/a dele)
her	(dela)	hers	(o/a dela)
its	(dele/a)	its	(o/a dele, dela)
our	(nosso/a)	ours	(o/a nosso/a)
your	(vosso/a)	yours	(o/a vosso/a)
their	(deles/as)	theirs	(o/a deles/as)

Possessivos concordam sempre com o possuidor e podem acompanhar ou substituir substantivos. Quando acompanham substantivos são adjetivos possessivos. Quando substituem substantivos são pronomes possessivos.

You love **your** contry, I love **mine**!
(adj.)   (pron.)

Em inglês possessivos não são precedidos por artigos.

Which coat do you prefer, **mine** or **hers**?

Exercises [answers on p. 207]

1 Classify the underlined possessive as Adj (adjective) or Pr (pronoun).

		Adj	Pr
1.	The little cat hurt its leg!	✓	
2.	Your copybooks are in the lab.		
3.	The car and the bike are hers.		
4.	Is that skate ours?		
5.	Josh and Terry are our friends.		

6. This book isn't <u>yours</u>. It's his.   ____ ____
7. Do you know <u>their</u> children?   ____ ____
8. Those schoolbags are <u>theirs</u>.   ____ ____
9. What is <u>his</u> name?   ____ ____

2 Check the correct alternative.

1. Who are those boys? Do you know _____ names?
   a. his   b. their ✓   c. theirs
2. Sandra lost her pen. Did Bill lost _____ ?
   a. his   b. hers   c. their
3. These are your shoes. Where are _____ ?
   a. mine   b. yours   c. my
4. That poor dog has broken _____ leg.
   a. hers   b. ours   c. its
5. _____ watch is out of order, but yours is not.
   a. Mine   b. My   c. Hers
6. Is _____ house on the right or on the left side?
   a. ours   b. hers   c. her
7. They don't want to give me _____ new magazine.
   a. hers   b. their   c. theirs
8. Whose bag is this: mine or _____ ?
   a. yours   b. your   c. her
9. Andres finished his work. Did Brenda finish _____ ?
   a. hers   b. her   c. their

3 Complete the sentence with the correct possessive.

1. We study near here. _____*Our*_____ school is amazing.
2. Bob likes singing with _____ mother.
3. My sister has sold _____ old car.
4. _____ car is black, although I don't like black.
5. Two of the boys didn't bring _____ books.
6. Those kids are Italian but _____ family is from Brazil.
7. Kate likes _____ grandfather.
8. Sue and Linda are going to school. _____ brother is going to the gym.
9. Roger is from France. _____ wife is from Italy.

63 Possessive of nouns ('s or ')

A forma **substantivo + 's/'** é usada para expressar posse, relação etc.

the mother**'s** voice   the boys**'** feet   the bird**s'** nests

1. + 's palavra não terminada em -s:		2. + ' palavra terminada em -s:	
possuidor	**coisa possuída**	**possuidor**	**coisa possuída**
the girl**'s**	blouse	the bus**'**	wheels
the lion**'s**	mane	the boys**'**	clothes
the men**'s**	books	the Browns**'**	house
Ann**'s**	pen	Achilles**'**	heel
my step-father**'s**	car	(nome clássico)	
John the Second**'s**	reign	obs: nomes comuns em **-s** recebem **'/ 's**: Jess**'** car ou Jess**'s** car	

Peculiarity – se houver mais de um possuidor:

para indicar posse comum último elemento + '/'s: Lucy and Bob**'s** father.	**para indicar posse individual** cada elemento + '/'s: Lucy**'s** and Bob**'s** fathers.

Notes – (a) '/'s é usado com pessoa, animal, meios de locomoção, lugares subentendidos, expressões de distância, tempo etc.: the dog's toys; the man's cup; the ship's crew; I'll go to Grandma's; an arm's length; a week's work; for goodness' sake.
(b) of é usado com coisas inanimadas, coletivos, com nomes geográficos, duplo possessivo: the legs of the table; the opinion of the public; the symbols of Paris; A friend of my brother's.; He is a friend of mine.

Exercises [answers on p. 207]

1 Supply ['] or ['s].

1. The men _'s_____ gloves.
2. The miners _____ boots
3. The sheep _____ ears.
4. The hunter _____ hat.

5. The dogs _____ puppies.
6. My mother _____ sister.
7. The birds _____ nest.
8. Adam _____ apple.
9. The puppy _____ ears.
10. My father _____ voice.
11. The children _____ toys.
12. The doctor _____ smile.
13. The ladies _____ glasses.
14. The bears _____ trail.
15. Jesus _____ disciples.
16. Dennis _____ room.

2 Rewrite sentences. Use ['] or ['s].

1. The restroom for the kid: The *kid's restroom.*
2. The car belonging to a friend: A _____
3. The house belonging to Gabriel: _____
4. The names of the twins: The _____
5. The name of your dog: My _____
6. The cats belonging to the girls: The _____
7. The tracks of the deer: The _____
8. The shoes belonging to Kat: _____

3 Supply ['s] or ['].

1. The soldiers '_____ boots were covered with mud.
2. Do you know the children _____ names?
3. When are the Browns _____ kids going to arrive?
4. Jason _____ mother and Tania _____ father got married yesterday.
5. The babies _____ mother said they are twins.
6. They are painting the doctor _____ office.
7. The Smiths _____ office is downtown.
8. Whales _____ milk is as thick as toothpaste.

64 Prefixes & Suffixes

Prefixos e **sufixos** são conjuntos de letras adicionados a uma palavra para formar novas palavras. **Prefixos** são adicionados ao início da palavra e **sufixos** ao final da palavra.

happy: **un**happy   **un**happi**ly**   happi**ness**   happi**ly**   **un**happi**ness**

Prefixos mais usados

prefix	meaning	example
de-	opposite	**de**frost, **de**code
dis-	not	**dis**agree, **dis**abled
in-, im-, il-, ir-	not	**in**justice, **il**legal
inter-	between	**inter**act, **inter**change
mis-	wrongly	**mis**lead, **mis**place
over-	over	**over**look, **over**do
re-	again	**re**turn, **re**act
sub-	under	**sub**marine, **sub**atom
trans-	across	**trans**port, **trans**form
un-	not	**un**do, **un**usual

Sufixos mais usados

suffix	meaning	example
-able, -ible	can be	comfort**able**, lov**able**
-ed	verb form	reach**ed**, paint**ed**
-er, -or	one who	paint**er**, act**or**
-ful	full of	care**ful**, pain**ful**
-ing	verb form	act**ing**, sing**ing**
-ion, -tion	act, process	attract**ion**, act**ion**
-less	without	home**less**, pain**less**
-ly	characteristic of	quick**ly**, soft**ly**
-ment	action, process	enjoy**ment**, agree**ment**
-ness	condition of	kind**ness**, happi**ness**
-s, -es	more than one	book**s**, box**es**
-y	characterized by	cloud**y**, wind**y**

Exercises [answers on p. 208]

1 Rewrite the words using the prefixes given.
1. view, related (inter-): _interview, interrelated_
2. available, clear (un-): _____
3. natural, tidy (un-): _____
4. fill, play (re-): _____
5. connect, appear (dis-): _____
6. correct, difference (in-): _____
7. form, forest (de-): _____
8. port, ocean (trans-): _____
9. spell, take (mis-): _____

2 Rewrite the words using the suffixes given.
1. care, harm (less): _careless, harmless_
2. fierce, peaceful (-ly): _____
3. noise, rain (-y): _____
4. do, employ (-er): _____
5. recycle, drink (-able): _____
6. dark, lazy (-ness): _____
7. truth, faith (-ful): _____
8. paint, read (-ing): _____
9. employ, move (-ment): _____

3 Add the correct prefix or suffix to the word given.

> un-   re-   dis-   mis-   -un   -er   -ing   -ful   -ly

1. (agree) I _____disagree_____ with you about this subject.
2. (lock) Could you _____ the door for her?
3. (open) The toy store will _____ next week.
4. (pack) _____ as soon as you arrive and come see us.
5. (use) It's _____ to carry some money in case of an emergency.
6. (usual) Is it _____ cold in October?
7. (interest) We believe this is an _____ subject to talk about.
8. (spell) We always _____ that word.
9. (sing) Kenny is the best _____ I know.

65 Prepositions

Preposições são palavras como *in, on, at, with* e *from*. São geralmente usadas antes de substantivos e pronomes mostrando a relação destes com outras palavras da frase.

The cat is sleeping **on** the table.   I came **on** foot.

Note – Prepositional phrase: é formada por uma preposição e um substantivo ou pronome que serve como objeto da preposição. She looked at me.

Preposições mais usadas.

about (sobre, em torno de)	talk **about** politics, walk **about** the town
above (acima de)	fly **above** the clouds
across (através)	run **across** the bridge
after (após)	meet **after** dinner
against (contra)	sail **against** the current
along (ao longo de, por)	walk **along** the road
among (entre, no meio de)	a man **among** his friends
around (ao redor, por)	walk **around** the block, leave **around** four
as (como)	work **as** a waiter, act **as** mediator
at (em – noite, hora; lugar)	**at** night, **at** seven, **at** school
before (antes, em frente)	**before** my house, **before** dinner
behind (atrás, depois de)	**behind** the door, **behind** the house
below (abaixo de)	**below** the surface, the words **below**
beside (ao lado de)	the tree **beside** the house
besides (além de)	buy a flat **besides** a car
between (entre 2)	sit **between** Jack and Jill, leave **between** 2:00 and 3:00
beyond (depois de, além de)	the river **beyond** the hill
but (exceto)	everyone **but** me
by (junto a, de, por)	**by** the sea, **by** bus, **by** Alex
concerning (a respeito de)	**concerning** our engagement
despite (apesar de)	swim **despite** the cold water
down (abaixo)	float **down** the river

during (durante)	sleep **during** the meeting
except (exceto)	everyone **except** my brother
for (por)	**for** six years, **for** you, **for** hours
from (de)	**from** Italy, **from** Jane
in (em: mês, dia, estação, ano, lugar)	**in** May, **in** the morning, **in** 2015, **in** an hour, **in** the kitchen
inside (dentro)	the car **inside** the garage
into (para dentro)	get **into** the house
like (como)	sing **like** a bird
near (perto, quase)	**near** here, **near** 5 years
of (de)	page **of** the book, glass **of** milk
off (fora de, para fora de)	fall **off** a cliff, eat **off** a dish
on (no, na; sobre)	**on** Monday, **on** the table, **on** the bus, **on** the beach
opposite (do lado oposto)	the house **opposite** the bank
out (para fora)	run **out** the door, drive **out** the park
outside (do lado de fora de)	go **outside** the city, stay **outside** the house
over (acima)	**over** the door, **over** our heads, **over** the river, **over** 2 years.
since (desde)	**since** 2001, **since** May, **since** childhood
than (do que)	faster **than** you, taller **than** me
through (através)	**through** the window, **through** the door
to (para)	go **to** bed, go **to** the cinema, go **to** Rome
toward/s (em direção a)	**towards** the house, **towards** the end of the year
under (embaixo, abaixo)	**under** the table, **under** 10 dollars
until (até)	dance **until** dawn, stay **until** Monday
up (contra, para o interior de)	row **up** the stream
upon (sobre)	climb **upon** my knee, the vase **upon** the table
with (com)	live **with** your friends, discuss **with** her, come **with** us
within (dentro de)	**within** one mile, **within** two days
without (sem)	**without** a car, **without** money

66 Preposition Combinations

Prepositions after verbs

Alguns verbos demandam o uso de certas preposições.

look **at**   listen **to**   agree **with**   dream **about**   believe **in**

Conheça algumas das associações:

accuse **of**	conceal **from**	listen **to**	search **for**
add **to**	concern **about**	live **at/in**	shout **at/to**
affix **to**	cooperate **with**	look **at**	shout **for**
agree **with**	depend **on**	name **after**	speak **to**
apply **for**	graduate **from**	participate **in**	talk **about**
apologize **for**	hear **about**	persevere **in**	talk **to**
approve **of**	hide **from**	point **at**	tell **about**
argue **with**	impress **on**	prepare **for**	think **abou/of**
arrive **at/in**	infer **from**	prevent **from**	trust **in**
ask **for**	insist **on**	protect **from**	vary **from**
believe **in**	invite **to** (place/event)	protest **against**	wait **for**
belong **to**	invite **for** (activity)	recover **from**	work **for**
blame **for**	knock **at**	rely **on**	worry **about**
borrow **from**	know **about**	return **to/from**	
bother **about**	laugh **at**	run **after**	
care **about**	learn **about**	run **from**	

Exercises [answers on p. 208]

1 Underline the correct preposition.
1. The forest guards protected us (<u>from</u>, of) the animals.
2. I learned (by, about) the whales.
3. The woman pointed (at, for) the thief.
4. Was he invited (of, to) the party?
5. This pill can prevent you (at, from) smoking.

6. What can we infer (by, from) his words?
7. He impressed it (on, at) silk screen.
8. This street was named (from, after) my grandfather.

2 Check the correct preposition.

1. You can borrow the book _____ the library.
   a. with   b. for   c. from ✓
2. He apologized _____ what he had said.
   a. to   b. for   c. at
3. We arrived _____ the club in the afternoon.
   a. about   b. with   c. at
4. Don't believe _____ what he says.
   a. at   b. in   c. about
5. I am concerned _____ my school grades.
   a. about   b. of   c. by
6. They cooperated _____ the policeman.
   a. with   b. by   c. for
7. Add it _____ the cost of the project.
   a. to   b. in   c. of
8. Did you argue _____ Tom?
   a. at   b. after   c. with
9. He concealed the truth _____ his mother.
   a. by   b. at   c. from
10. The man was accused _____ the crime.
    a. from   b. by   c. of

3 Supply the correct preposition.

1. They had to run _____ *after* _____ their dogs
2. "Trust _____ God", he said.
3. You should not rely _____ her.
4. Prices may vary _____ day to day.
5. Mom recovered _____ a bad cold.
6. Don't shout _____ me.
7. The children shouted _____ help.
8. They are going to protest _____ food prices.
9. Return the book _____ me after you read it.
10. They searched _____ a prisoner.

67 Present Tenses I

General table

Vários tempos verbais podem expressar ações do tempo presente ou que têm alguma relação com o presente.

I **live** in Brazil.
I **am doing** my exercises.
I **have studied** a lot.
I **have been studying** English.

verb tense	expresses
present simple verbo (+s/es)	verdade geral, fato, ação repetida, hábito, emoção, sentimento, ação futura: Ice **floats** on water. I **like** coffee. The train **leaves** at six every week. Your test **starts** at seven. We can talk when you **come** back.
present progressive am/is/are + v.-ing[1]	ação acontecendo no momento, ação futura: I **am getting** better. He **is studying** in his room now. He **is retiring** next year.
present perfect have/has + v. pp[2]	ação iniciada no passado e ainda acontecendo: I **have waited** for 2 hours.[3] She **has moved** to London.
present perfect progressive have/has been + v.-ing	ênfase da duração da ação: I **have been waiting** for hours. She **has been cooking** all day.

Note – **(1) Abreviations: v.** = verbo **pp** = past participle; **(2)** o **Present Perfect** e o **Present Perfect Progressive** são tempos que podem fazer referência ao presente e ao passado.
(3) Traduções: Espero há duas horas; Ela mudou para Londres; Estou esperando há horas; Ela esteve cozinhando o dia todo.

Exercises [answers on p. 209]

1 Identify the types of action.

a. general truth, fact, repeated action
b. ongoing action
c. future action
d. focus in the action
e. connection to present

1. I don't live in Rio, I live in São Paulo. _____a_____
2. We have been studying hard. _____
3. The team is arriving in two hours. _____
4. The children are sleeping now. _____
5. Mom arrives tomorrow. _____
6. He meets his friends on Fridays. _____
7. Water freezes below zero. _____
8. They have worked here since April. _____

2 Check the correct alternative.

1. They usually _____ television in the evening.
   a. have watched   b. are watching   c. watch ✓
2. We _____ the bus every morning.
   a. have been   b. catch   c. be catching
3. Our holiday _____ on July 1st.
   a. starts   b. has start   c. start
4. He _____ to Oxford next winter.
   a. has been moving   b. is moving   c. has moved
5. She only _____ fish.
   a. is eaten   b. eats   c. has eating
6. They never _____ buses.
   a. drive   b. has drive   c. is driving
7. This summer _____ too slowly.
   a. have passed   b. pass   c. is passing
8. We'll give it to her when she _____.
   a. arrives   b. has arrived   c. arrive

68 Present Tenses II

Present progressive

O *present progressive* expressa ações em andamento na atualidade ou no momento da fala. Pode ser usado também para expressar ações futuras. É usado com palavras como: *now, at this moment, at present* etc.:

I **am studying** now.
He **is sleeping** now.

Jill **is coming** next week.
They **are working** at present.

Present Progressive (be + v.-ing)	
to walk – affirmative	
I **am**	We **are**
You **are** walking.	You **are** walking.
He, She, It **is**	They **are**

Forms	
interrogative: **Is** he walking?	question: **Where** is he walking?
negative: He is **not** walking.	short answer: Yes, he **is**. No, he **isn't**.
negative-interrogative: **Isn't** he walking?	contracted form: is not: **isn't** are not: **aren't**

Spelling

Ao receber **-ing** a maioria dos verbos não sofre alteração:

do – do**ing**   buy – buy**ing**,   porém, verbo terminado em:

1. e:	2. ie:	3. c.v.c[1] (sílaba tônica):
perde o -e	y	dobra a consoante
rid**e** – rid**ing**	d**ie** – d**y**ing	run – ru**nn**ing begin – begi**nn**ing
writ**e** – writ**ing**	l**ie** – l**y**ing	occur – occu**rr**ing

Note – (1) c/v/c: consoante/ vogal/ consoante

P | 143

Exercises [answers on p. 209]

1 Write sentences in the present progressive. Use the words given.

1. (she/ run/ the park) *She is running in the park.*
2. (we/ not begin/ the exercise) _____
3. (I/ not do/ the dishes) _____
4. (Paul/ write/ a song/ ?) _____
5. (boy/ not lie) _____
6. (children/ play/ soccer/ ?) _____
7. (you/ ride/ a bike/ ?) _____
8. (the phone/ ring/ ?) _____

2 Complete the sentences with the present progressive of the verbs given.

1. (not swim, study) The boys *aren't swimming* they *'re studying*.
2. (lie) I don't believe you. I know you _____.
3. (play) _____ Jeff _____ tennis at the club?
4. (cut) Why _____ Sandra _____ bread?
5. (not ring) The phone _____. It's your imagination.
6. (write) Usher and David _____ messages to their friends.
7. (study) Where _____ they _____?
8. (leave) _____ you _____ now?

3 Match questions and answers.

a. She doesn't want to go to bed.
b. Yes, they are.
c. No, he isn't.
d. At home.
e. I am making a cake.
f. Yes, I am.
g. To the manager.
h. They are playing soccer.

1. Are you late for the concert? — *f*
2. What are they doing at this moment? ___
3. Why is the Rachel crying? ___
4. Is Tom working at present? ___
5. Where is Karen studying? ___
6. Are the girls arriving tomorrow? ___
7. Who are the workers talking to? ___
8. What are you doing right now? ___

69 Present Tenses III

Present simple

O **Presente Simples** é usado para expressar ações rotineiras, verdades universais e fatos; pode também expressar ações futuras.

Geralmente é usado com palavras como:
always, never, sometimes, usually, often, everyday, rarely etc.

I **study** everyday.   Ice **floats** on water.   Mom **arrives** tomorrow.

Present Simple (v. + s/es)
to work – affirmative
I **work.**	He, She, It **works.**	You **work.**
You **work.**	We **work.**	They **work.**

Forms	
interrogative: **Do** you work? **Does** he work? negative: I **do not** work. He **does not** work. negative-interrogative: **Don't** you work? **Doesn't** he work?	question: **Where** do you work? **Where** does he work? short answer: Yes, I **do.** No, I **don't.** Yes, he **does.** No, he **doesn't.** contracted form: do not: **don't** does not: **doesn't**

Note – o verbo principal fica no infinitivo **sem to** quando usado com o auxiliar **do/does**.

Spelling

No presente simples, a 3ª pessoa do singular da maioria dos verbos recebe apenas **-s:**

play**s**   write**s**   cut**s**   exceto   have → **has**

Porém, verbo terminado em:

1. o, ss, sh, ch, x **ou** z	2. **consoante** + y
recebe es:	y muda para i + es:
goes misses rushes	copy – cop**ies** dry – dr**ies**
catches mixes buzzes	hurry – hurr**ies** study – stud**ies**

Exercises [answers on p. 210]

1 Rewrite the sentence according to the information given.

1. (neg.) I work near my house.   *I don't work near my house.*
2. (int.) John sleeps early.   _____
3. (aff.) Do they always get late?   _____
4. (int.) He often washes his car.   _____
5. (neg.) Sheila studies French.   _____

2 Supply the correct form of the verb given.

1. (miss) She _____ *misses* _____ the bus everyday.
2. (rush) _____ Tom always _____ to school?
3. (go) Cliff usually _____ to work by car.
4. (catch) My sister rarely _____ that bus.
5. (not brush) Paul _____ his teeth after lunch.

3 Underline the correct verb form.

1. Sheila (speak, <u>speaks</u>) English well.
2. They (watches, don't watch) TV in the evening.
3. (Do, Does) the bus usually (stops, stop) here?
4. My brother (doesn't dance, doesn't dances) well.
5. Where (do, does) your friends (live, lives)?
6. Alice and Ron (drives, don't drive) to work everyday.
7. What (does, do) your friend (like, likes) to read?
8. I rarely (drink, doesn't drink) milk.

4 Answer the questions.

1. Where do you go on weekends? *I go to...* _____
2. When do you study? _____
3. Do you go to school on foot or by car? _____
4. How does your best friend go to school? _____

70 Present Tenses IV

Present perfect and past simple

O **Passado Simples** expressa ação passada em tempo claramente determinado.

I **bought** a car **last week**.   I **saw him yesterday**.

O **Presente Perfeito**[1], expressa:
→ ação ocorrida no passado cujo tempo não é mencionado; ação repetida.
I have bought a car!   I 've seen him many times.
(Comprei um carro!)   (Eu o vi muitas vezes.)

→ ação iniciada no passado e que continua ocorrendo no presente.
I have been sick since yesterday. (Estou doente desde ontem.)

O **Presente Perfeito** é usado com palavras como:
ever, never, since, for, already, yet, just, many times, lately etc.
I **have already done** the exercises.   He **has worked** hard lately.
(Já fiz os exercícios.)   (Ele tem trabalhado muito ultimamente.)

Present Perfect (have/has + v. pp[2])	
to leave – affirmative	
I, We, You, They **have left**.	He, She, It **has left**.

Forms			
interrogative:		question:	
Have they left?	**Has** he left?	**Why** have you left?	**Why** has he left?
negative:		short answer:	
They **have not** left.	He **has not** left.	Yes, I **have**.	No, I **haven't**.
negative-interrogative:		Yes, he **has**.	No, he **hasn't**.
Haven't you left?	**Hasn't** he left?	contracted form:	
		have: **'ve**	has: **'s**
		has not: **hasn't**	have not: **haven't**

Notes – **(1)** a tradução desse tempo verbal depende do contexto. **(2) v.** = verbo; **pp.** = past participle.

Exercises [answers on p. 210]

1 Rewrite the sentences according to the information given.

1. (neg.) I have seen David recently. *I haven't seen Dave recently.*
2. (int.) He has studied Greek. _____
3. (who) They have talked to Kevin. _____
4. (where) I have lived in India. _____
5. (aff.) Have they moved to Rio? _____
6. (aff.) We haven't bought a house. _____
7. (int.) Julia has come from Japan. _____
8. (neg.) We have had lunch at home. _____

2 Supply the present perfect tense of the verbs given.

1. (write) I ____*have*____ already ____*written*____ the letter.
2. (work) He _____ here for two weeks.
3. (go) We _____ to London many times.
4. (be) _____ you ever _____ to Canada?
5. (visit) They _____ me recently.
6. (not see) I _____ Paul lately.
7. (live) Susan _____ in Greece.
8. (not arrive) The boys _____ yet.

3 Complete the sentences with the correct tense of the verbs given.

1. (be) We ____*have been*____ on vacation for the last 15 days.
2. (be) We _____ on vacation 15 days ago.
3. (break) Sue _____ her leg!
4. (break) Sue _____ her leg last night.
5. (finish) He _____ his work one hour ago.
6. (finish) _____ you _____ your homework?
7. (buy) I _____ my book yesterday.
8. (buy) I _____ my English book!

148 | P

71 Present Tenses V

Present perfect & present perfect progressive

O *Present Perfect* pode ser usado com:

already (já)	Has he **already** gone? He has **already** gone. (Ele já saiu.)
ever (alguma vez)	Have you **ever** been to Rio? (Você já esteve no Rio?)
for (por)	I've been there **for** ten days. (Estive lá por dez dias.)
just (ação recente)	He has **just** arrived. (Ele acaba de chegar)
many times (muitas vezes)	I've met him **many times**. (Eu o encontrei muitas vezes.)
never (nunca)	She has **never** lied to me. (Ela nunca mentiu para mim.)
lately (ultimamente)	I've slept well **lately**. (Tenho dormido bem ultimamente.)
recently (recentemente)	He has worked hard recently. (Ele tem trabalhado muito recentemente.)
since (desde)	They've lived here **since** June. (Eles moram aqui desde junho.)
yet (já, ainda)	Has he finished dinner **yet**? (Ele já terminou o jantar?) He hasn't finished dinner **yet**. (Ele ainda não terminou o jantar.)

O *Present Perfect Progressive* **(have/has been + v. -ing)** enfatiza a duração da ação. Sua tradução depende do contexto.

He **has been talking** for hours.
(Ele está falando há horas.)

You **have been lying** to me.
(Você tem mentido para mim.)

Exercises [answers on p. 211]

1 **Turn into Portuguese.**

1. You have lied to me many times.
   _____

2. We have traveled by train lately.
   _____

3. James and Kate have just moved.
   _____

2 **Rewrite the adverb in the correct place.**

1. (since) I have _____ met many people ___*since*___ I arrived.
2. (recently) He has _____ been sleeping well _____ .
3. (yet) We haven't _____ seen Laura _____ .
4. (ever) Have you _____ been to Petra _____ ?
5. (never) He has _____ visited _____ us.
6. (just) They have _____ got married _____ .
7. (already) Has Linda _____ arrived _____ ?
8. (many times) I have _____ seen that movie _____ .

3 **Check the correct alternative.**

1. We _____ to the new place yet.
   a. haven't moved ✓   b. didn't move   c. have moved
2. He _____ an apartment recently.
   a. has bought   b. bought   c. didn't buy
3. _____ you _____ Tom yet?
   a. Haven't – seen   b. Do – see   c. Have – been seen
4. That boy _____ the window.
   a. broke   b. has been breaking   c. has broken
5. The children _____ to bed late last night.
   a. have gone   b. went   c. haven't gone
6. We _____ already _____ about that!
   a. didn't – talk   b. have – talking   c. have – talked
7. My brother _____ a lot recently.
   a. worked   b. has been working   c. has working
8. Somebody _____ my bag.
   a. stole   b. has stolen   c. didn't steal

72 Quantifiers

Much, many etc.

Quantificadores são palavras como *much e many* e expressam alguma forma de quantidade. Alguns antecedem substantivos contáveis[1] (countable nouns), outros antecedem substantivos incontáveis[2] (uncountable nouns).

many cars   **few** books   **much** coffee   **little** salt

for countable nouns[3]		for uncountable nouns	
many	(muitos,as)	much	(muito/a)
few	(poucos/as)	little	(pouco/a)
a few	(alguns/mas)	a little	(algum/a)
fewer	(menos)	less	(menos)
a lot of, lots of, plenty of (muito/a/os/as)			

They speak **many** languages.   I don't have **much** money.
We took **a few** pictures.   There is **little** time left.

You have **plenty of** time.   There's **a lot of** beer.   She gets **lots of** friends.

Notes – (1) Countable Nouns: nomeiam coisas que podem ser contadas: cars, trees etc.;
(2) Uncountable Nouns: nomeiam coisas que não podem ser contadas: air, love etc.
(3) ver Countable & Uncountable Nouns p. 51.

Exercises [answers on p. 211]

1 Complete the sentences with *much* or *many*.

1. He didn't invite _____ *many* _____ people for his play.
2. He drank _____ wine and couldn't walk home.
3. You have plenty of time but I haven't _____.

Q | 151

4. _____ girls wore long dresses last night.
5. I received _____ emails last week.
6. He ate _____ pasta and felt horrible.
7. Did you take _____ pictures?
8. Did you buy a lot of books? Yes, _____.

2 **Complete the sentences with or little or few.**
1. There is _____*little*_____ possibility of success.
2. Did you spend _____ money on food?
3. Alice invited just a _____ friends for dinner.
4. She has _____ coins in her pocket.
5. I need a _____ money for the gas.
6. _____ people understand what he says.
7. Smoking is one of my _____ bad habits.
8. There are a lot of carrots and a _____ potatoes.

3 **Check the correct alternative.**
1. They will call _____*fewer*_____ than four students.
   a. much   b. fewer   c. many
2. I haven't been to NY _____ times.
   a. many   b. less   c. little
3. _____ workers have large families.
   a. Little   b. Few   c. Much
4. They have so _____ money that they can't pay for their rent.
   a. much   b. many   c. little
5. 5. She gets lots of friends but I don't get _____.
   a. much   b. little   c. many
6. I don't spend _____ money on magazines.
   a. many   b. few   c. much
7. You should spend _____ time on shopping.
   a. few   b. less   c. many
8. You can buy _____ cheese than ham for the sandwiches.
   a. much   b. less   c. little

73 Questions

Direct & indirect (embedded)

Podemos fazer perguntas de forma direta (direct question) ou indireta (indirect or embedded question).

Direct questions
Perguntas diretas são informais, feitas sem rodeios, normalmente dirigidas a parentes e amigos. Dependendo da situação, podem ser consideradas rudes. A forma é a interrogativa.

Who are you going to invite?   Where's the bathroom?
What did he tell you?   When is he going away?

Indirect/embedded questions
Perguntas indiretas são mais polidas e formais, usualmente dirigidas a pessoas menos conhecidas. São chamadas indiretas porque ficam na forma afirmativa. São precedidas por perguntas ou frases como:

Can you tell me...   Could you tell me...
Do you have any idea...   Do you know...
I wonder...   I'd like to know...
Is there any chance...   Would it be possible...

Direct →	Indirect
Who **are you** going to invite?	*I wonder* who **you are** going to invite.
What **did he** tell you?	*Can you tell me* what **he told** you?
Where**'s the bathroom**?	*I'd like to know* where **the bathroom is**.
When **is he** going away?	*Do you know* when **he is** going away?
Where **does he** live?	*Could you tell me* where **he lives**?

Note – Perguntas indiretas também são usadas em **Reported Speech**.
Where do you live? → I asked him where he lived.

Exercises [answers on p. 212]

1 Check the correct indirect question.

1. Where is the bank?
   a. Do you know where the bank is? ✓
   b. Where is the bank, do you know?
2. What time is it?
   a. Can you tell me what time is it?
   b. Could you tell me what time it is?
3. When does the bus arrive?
   a. Do you know when the bus arrives?
   b. I wonder when does the bus arrive?
4. What did they tell you?
   a. I'd like to know what did they tell you.
   b. I wonder what they told you.
5. Will they come?
   a. Do you know if will they come?
   b. I wonder if they will come.

2 Complete the sentence to transform the question into indirect question.

1. Why did they move to Brazil?
   I was wondering *why they moved to Brazil* .
2. How has she managed to get so rich?
   Do you have any idea _____?
3. How much does that skate cost?
   I'd like to know _____ .
4. What time did the plane land?
   Can you tell me _____?
5. Could we meet next Friday?
   I wonder if _____ .
6. Where is Oxford Street?
   Could you tell me _____?
7. What did she want?
   Do you know _____?
8. Who arrived?
   Do you know _____?

74 Reflexive Pronouns

Pronomes reflexivos caracterizam-se pelas terminações **-self/-selves**. Concordam com o substantivo ou com o pronome ao qual se referem e podem exercer diferentes funções.

personal pronouns	reflexive pronouns	
I	my**self**	(me, eu mesmo)
You	your**self**	(te, tu/você mesmo)
He	him**self**	(se, ele mesmo)
She	her**self**	(se, ela mesma)
It	it**self**	(se, ele/a mesmo/a)
We	our**selves**	(nos, nós mesmos)
You	your**selves**	(vos, vós/vocês mesmos)
They	them**selves**	(se, eles mesmos)

1. função reflexiva	2. função enfática	3. função idiomática
A ação recaí sobre o sujeito: I hurt **myself**. We cut **ourselves**.	Enfatiza um elemento da frase: I saw **Bob himself**. **I myself** talked to him. I talked to him **myself**.	Indica: sozinho, sem ajuda. I did the exercise **by myself**. He built the boat **by himself**.

Note – Um pronome reflexivo não atua como sujeito: Tom and I saw you (e não: Tom and myself saw you).

Exercises [answers on p. 212]

Classify the underlined pronoun as R (reflexive), E (emphatic) or I (idiomatic).

1. They talked to themselves.   _R_
2. He lives by himself.   ____
3. She made the dress herself.   ____
4. I talked to the President himself.   ____
5. The dog hurt itself under the bench.   ____

6. Bob has introduced himself to the teacher. _____
7. We ourselves painted the house. _____
8. Do you always talk to yourself? _____

2 Underline the correct alternative.
1. Amy blames (itself, <u>herself</u>) for the accident.
2. Where did he cut (himself, herself)?
3. They dogs ate all the food (themselves, itself).
4. The boys (himself, themselves) did most of the work.
5. Sometimes I prefer to be by (itself, myself).
6. Susan, you should look after (yourself, yourselves).
7. The house (herself, itself) was so dirty that we couldn't stay there.
8. We enjoyed (yourselves, ourselves) at the park.

3 Supply the correct reflexive pronoun.
1. I thought to _____*myself*_____ : What a day!
2. I can't leave the girl by _____ . She's too young.
3. He looked at _____ in the mirror.
4. We like cleaning the house _____ .
5. Ben and Jess defended _____ perfectly.
6. Is that old man talking to _____ ?
7. They _____ promised to come to our party.
8. She mailed the letter to _____ .

75 Relative Pronouns I

Who, which, that etc.

Pronomes relativos são palavras como *who, which, that* etc. Um pronome relativo introduz uma oração subordinada que, por sua vez, traz informações sobre um elemento da oração principal.

O pronome relativo a ser usado depende:

→ de sua função na oração subordinada: sujeito, objeto
→ da palavra que o antecede: pessoa, coisa, lugar.

antecedent	Subject	Object
people	who, that	who(m), that, xx
things	which, that	which, that, xx
places	where, in which	
(possessive)	whose	

		(oração subordinada)
subject		
people:	I helped a **man**	who/that was sick.
things:	I helped a **dog**	which/that was sick.
object		
people:	I saw the **girl**	who/that/xx you love.
things:	I sold the **book**	which/that/xx you saw.
place		
	I know the **town**	where he lives.
possessive		
	I helped a man	whose leg was broken.
	I helped the dog	whose leg was broken.

Note – whom é usado para pessoas e depois de preposições: *The man to whom you talked is my brother.*

Exercises [answers on p. 212]

1 Classify the relative pronoun in the underlined sentence as S (subject) or O (object)

1. He is the man <u>who is my neighbor</u>.   _S_
2. Yesterday I saw a bag <u>which was very expensive</u>.   ___
3. The man <u>who you saw near the door</u> is my teacher.   ___
4. This is the house <u>that was on fire</u>.   ___
5. This is the house <u>which I've built</u>.   ___
6. The people <u>who arrived</u> are hungry.   ___
7. The woman to <u>whom I was talking</u> is an actress.   ___
8. Have you seen the cat <u>that is hurt</u>?   ___

2 Underline the correct pronouns to complete the sentences.

1. Do you know the girl (whose, <u>who</u>) brought the mail?
2. That is the woman (who, whose) husband broke both legs.
3. I can't find the camera (who, that) you lent me yesterday.
4. He brought me the books (xx, whose) I needed.
5. That's the hospital (where, whom) I was born.
6. Tell us about the place (who, xx) you were born.
7. I don't know to (which/whom) he gave the flowers.
8. I like games (that, who) have a lot of action.
9. The house (which, xx) is across the street was sold out.
10. She delivered the letter (which, whose) was in a blue envelope.

3 Complete the sentences with all possible relative pronouns.

1. This is the town _____ _where/in which_ _____ the people live in caves.
2. This is the town _____ people live in caves.
3. The girls _____ you know live near my house.
4. The car _____ he wants to buy is very expensive.
5. He is the teacher _____ helped us solve the problem.
6. The apples _____ I bought are fresh.
7. He has books _____ he will never read.
8. He is the man _____ son caused the accident.
9. The doctor _____ talked to me was very kind.
10. They got on the bus _____ was going south.

76 Relative Pronouns II

Relative clauses

Pronomes relativos como *who, that, which* etc. introduzem orações subordinadas (relative clauses). Tais orações fornecem informação sobre o elemento ao qual se referem na oração principal (main clause).

(relative clause)
He is **the man who stole my watch**.
(subject)

(relative clause)
The dog that I saw was hurt.
(object)

A *Relative Clause* pode ser restritiva ou explicativa.

1. defining (restritiva)	2. non-defining (explicativa)
→ é essencial para a compreensão de seu antecedente.	→ não é essencial para a compreensão do antecedente.
→ admite o uso de **that**.	→ não admite **that**.
→ admite a omissão do pronome relativo (objeto).	→ não admite a omissão de pronomes.
→ não vem entre vírgulas.	→ vem depois de ou entre vírgulas.
I saw the man **(that) you love**.	My dog, **which is cute,** loves you.

Observe os pronomes usados em cada caso.

	defining	non-defining
Subject	people: **who, that** things: **which, that**	people: **who** things: **which**
Object	people: **who(m), that, xx** things: **which, that, xx**	people: **who(m)** things: **which**
	places: **where, in which** possessive: **whose**	

Note – **That** é o relativo usado depois de superlativos, indefinidos e diferentes antecedentes:

He is the best boy that I know; I know the man and the dog that were hurt.

Exercises [answers on p. 213]

Classify the underlined clause as D (defining) or ND (non-defining).

1. He is the man that helped me.   _D_
2. Tom, who is my classmate, helped me.   ____
3. France, which is his country, will accept him back.   ____
4. She is the girl whose sister lives is Thailand.   ____
5. Sandra, who you know very well, is not coming.   ____
6. My son, whose work is dangerous, is back home.   ____
7. My house, which is in Denver, is very small.   ____
8. The wolf which attacked him ran to the woods.   ____

Complete the sentences with all possible relative pronouns.

1. I helped the man _____ who/that _____ was sick.
2. Alex, _____ is not very young, is my brother.
3. This car, _____ runs really fast, costs over $300,000.
4. The woman _____ lives next door works as a teacher.
5. The film _____ we saw last week was awful.
6. This is the skirt _____ I bought yesterday.
7. The boy _____ you saw is my brother.
8. My grandmother, _____ is 93, swims every day.
9. I've just seen Helen, _____ husband works in Goa.
10. My mother, _____ is a nice person, will talk to you.

Complete the sentences with all possible relative pronouns.

1. Jim, _____ who _____ lives in NY, sent me a postcard.
2. The new skate, _____ I bought last week, is great.
3. Billy Paul, _____ brother is a singer, hates singing.
4. This is the place _____ I saw the thief.
5. Barcelona, _____ I like very much, is a beautiful song.
6. That is the house _____ they live.
7. My car, _____ is not expensive, is in the garage.
8. J. C. Foster, _____ is a famous actor, lives across the street.
9. Mary and Ann, _____ you know, moved to LA.
10. That tree, _____ bent down, had plenty of fruit.

77 Reported (Indirect) Speech

Para relatar o que alguém disse podemos usar **discurso direto** ou **indireto**:

direct speech – quando repetimos exatamente o que foi dito.
reported speech – quando contamos o que foi dito.

Ann: I love you. → She said, **"I love you."** (direct speech)
→ She **said (that) she loved me.** (reported speech)

O **discurso indireto** é introduzido por verbos como *say (that), tell, ask*, requer mudanças de tempo verbal[1], pronomes, algumas palavras e (em perguntas) mudança na ordem das palavras.

Direct speech	Reported speech
Present; Present Progressive He said, "I am tired." "I am reading."	**Past; Past Progressive** He said (that) he **was** tired. he **was reading**.
Past/Present Perfect/Past Progressive He said, "I bought it." "I have arrived." "I was jogging.	**Past Perfect/Past Perfect Progressive** He said he **had bought** it. he **had arrived**. he **had been jogging**.
Future He said, "I will study all night."	**Conditional** He said he **would study** all night.
Imperative He said, "(Don't) Open it."	**Infinitive** He told me **(not) to open** it.
Modal He said, "I could go."	**Modal** He said he **could** go.
Questions He said, "Do you like her?" "What time is it?"	He asked **if I liked her.** **what time it was.**

Notes – (1) Outras mudanças: can → could; must → have to; this / these → that / those; here → there; now → then; today → that day; yesterday → the day before; tomorrow → the following day. **(2) não há mudança do tempo: (a)** com fatos ainda válidos – He said the Earth is round; **(b)** se o tempo usado para relatar estiver no present simple, present perfect ou future – He says the test is easy.

Exercises [answers on p. 213]

1 Supply the correct verb tense.

1. "I saw him." → She said that she ___*had seen*___ him.
2. "There's a fly in my soup!" → I said _____ a fly in my soup!
3. "I'll see you later." → She said she _____ me later.
4. "I don't know!" → He said he _____.
5. "We are happy." → They told me they _____ happy.
6. "Can I go out now?" → He asked me if he _____ out then.
7. "I've painted the door." → He said he _____ the door.
8. "I'll sing tomorrow." → He said he _____ the following day.
9. "I have already been there." → He said _____ there.
10. "Did they invite you?" → He asked if they _____ me.

2 Rewrite the sentences. Use reported speech.

1. "What time will you be home?"
   He asked *what time I would go home.*
2. "Does she like coffee?"
   He asked if _____
3. "Why did he leave?"
   She asked me _____
4. "Leave the room, boys."
   He told _____
5. The baby was laughing.
   She said that _____

3 Rewrite the sentences in the reported speech form.
(note: verb tenses need no change).

1. "It is raining."
   She says *it is raining.*
2. "The Earth moves round the sun."
   He said that _____
3. "Honesty is the best policy."
   The teacher told us that _____
4. "The Hindus burn their dead."
   He told me that _____

78 Spelling and Pronunciation

Final s/es, er/est, d/ed, ing

Spelling	
1. final -s/-es A maioria das palavras recebe -s. days trees books buys plays loves palavra terminada em s, ss, sh, ch, x, z, o recebe -es: buses bushes peaches boxes quizzes heroes misses rushes catches mixes buzzes goes palavra em consoante/y troca o y por i + es: city – cities lady – ladies dry – dries hurry – hurries study – studies	**2. final -er/-est** A maioria das palavras não sofre alteração e as terminadas em e perdem essa letra. tall taller tallest large larger largest palavra em consoante/y troca o y para i. happy happier happiest angry angrier angriest palavra em consoante/vogal/consoante: dobra a consoante: hot hotter hottest thin thinner thinnest
3. final -d/-ed A maioria dos verbos não sofre alteração e os terminados em e perdem essa letra like – liked enjoy – enjoyed live – lived play – played verbo terminado em consoante/y: troca o y para i. carry – carried study – studied hurry – hurried verbo terminado em sílaba tônica consoante/vogal/consoante: dobra a consoante. stop – stopped occur – occurred prefer – preferred	**4. final -ing** A maioria das palavras não sofre alteração e as terminadas em e perdem essa letra. buy – buying ride – riding study – studying have – having do – doing take – taking Mas... be – being verbo em ie: troca ie por y. die – dying tie – tying lie – lying verbo terminado em sílaba tônica consoante/vogal/consoante: dobra a consoante. run – running begin – beginning occur – occurring

Pronunciation

1. final -s/es
tem som de /iz/ após os sons:
s, z, sh, ch, j.
misses   rises   wishes
watches judges washes

/s/ após os sons: p, t, k, f, h[1]
stops   hits   packs
laugh   takes talks

/z/ após vogais e demais sons
(b, g, j, l, m, n, r, th, v, z[2])
rides   pays   bags
loves   rains dreams

2. final -d/ed
tem som de /id/ após os sons: d, t
needed   added   waited
visited repeated

/t/ após: k, f, p, s, ch, sh, th[1]
looked   pushed   asked
watched helped   dressed

/d/ após vogais e demais sons
(b, g, j, l, m, n, r, th, v, z.[2])
sobbed   roamed   believed
judged   filled   enjoyed

Notes – **(1) unvoiced sound** – as cordas vocais não vibram. **(2) voiced** – as cordas vocais vibram.

79 Tag Question

Tag Question é uma pequena pergunta – afirmativa ou negativa – feita com a finalidade de pedir uma confirmação para algo dito. Com frases afirmativas usamos *tag questions* negativas. Com frases negativas usamos *tag questions* afirmativas.

He is fine, **isn't he?**   He isn't fine, **is he?**

Form
(auxiliary verb + pronoun)

1. frase afirmativa

tag question negativa:*
You are tired, **aren't you?**
Joe is sleeping, **isn't he?**
Kate was late, **wasn't she?**
They were crying, **weren't they?**
You work, **don't you?**
He studies, **doesn't he?**
Ann cried, **didn't she?**
Paul has arrived, **hasn't he?**
You have slept, **haven't you?**
They had left, **hadn't they?**
Bob can swim, **can't he?**
You could rest, **couldn't you?**
They will come, **won't they?**
You would help, **wouldn't you?**
He should leave, **shouldn't he?**
We might go, **mightn't we?**

formas irregulares:
I'm late, **aren't I?**
We may go now, **may we not?**
You never cry, **do you?**
There is a dog here, **isn't there?**

2. frase negativa

tag question afirmativa:
You aren't sick, **are you?**
Joe isn't sleeping, **is he?**
Kate wasn't late, **was she?**
They weren't jogging, **were they?**
You don't work, **do you?**
He doesn't study, **does he?**
Ann didn't cry, **did she?**
Paul hasn't arrived, **has he?**
You haven't slept, **have you?**
They hadn't left, **had they?**
Bob can't swim, **can he?**
You couldn't rest, **could you?**
They won't come, **will they?**
You wouldn't help, **would you?**
He shouldn't leave, **should he?**
We mightn't go, **might we?**
I may not go, **may I?**

formas irregulares:
Let's go, **shall we?**
(Don't) talk here, **will you?**
There aren't any dogs here, **are there?**

Note – **tag question negativa* é feita com auxiliar na forma negativa e abreviada.

Exercises [answers on p. 214]

1 Check the correct tag question.

1. Your sister was studying, _____ wasn't she _____?
   a. wasn't sister   b. was she   c. wasn't she ✓
2. The teacher didn't see us, _____?
   a. did she?   b. didn't he?   c. doesn't she
3. You were late yesterday, _____?
   a. weren't you?   b. did you   c. were you
4. Rachel and Tom haven't arrived, _____?
   a. wasn't she?   b. has he?   c. have they
5. They won't come, _____?
   a. will they   b. isn't it?   c. do they
6. You can speak Italian, _____?
   a. can you?   b. don't you   c. can't you
7. Your brother works at home, _____?
   a. doesn't he?   b. has she?   c. does he
8. We should visit Kate, _____?
   a. shouldn't she?   b. shouldn't we   c. don't we
9. Alice saw the accident yesterday, _____?
   a. did Alice   b. didn't Alice   c. didn't she
10. I am intelligent, _____?
    a. don't I   b. aren't I   c. am not

2 Supply the correct tag questions.

1. Marion didn't arrive on time, _____ did she _____?
2. Julie and Carol love you, _____?
3. We had had dinner when they arrived, _____?
4. You will always be my best friend, _____?
5. The Wilsons haven't built the house yet, _____?
6. Our father should sell that old car, _____?
7. The children were watching TV when you arrived, _____?
8. Let's talk to her tomorrow, _____?
9. You mother cooks well, _____?
10. Grace is a nurse at this hospital, _____?

80 There to be

Present & past

There to be (= haver, existir) é usado para indicar a existência ou quantidade de algo.

There is an apple in the box.
There were cats outside.
There will be a great show next week.

affirmative	present	past	future
singular	**there is** (há)	**there was** (havia, houve)	**there will be** (haverá)
plural	**there are** (há)	**there were** (havia, houve)	

Forms	
interrogative: **Is** there a dog here? **Were** there dogs here? **Will** there be dogs here? negative: There is **not** a dog here. There were **not** dogs here. There will **not** be dogs here. negative-interrogative: **Isn't** there a dog here? **Weren't** there dogs here? **Won't** there be dogs here?	question: **Where** is there a dog? **How many** dogs were there? **What** will there be next year? short answer: Yes, there **is**. No, there **isn't**. Yes, there **are**. No, there **aren't**. Yes, there **were**. No, there **weren't**. Yes, there **will be**. No, there **won't be**. contracted form: there is: **there's** there are: — there will be: **there'll be** there is not: **there isn't** there are not: **there aren't** there was not: **there wasn't** there were not: **there weren't** there will not: **there won't be**

Note – Posse: a ideia de posse é transmitida por **to have** (= ter). Ex: I have a dog.

Exercises [answers on p. 214]

1 **Complete the sentences with the present forms of there to be.**
1. _____There is_____ a taxi in front of the house!
2. _____ room for me in your car?
3. _____ many people at his party because he has few friends.
4. _____ anything I can do for you?
5. Take some of the apples. _____ many!

2 **Complete the sentences with the past forms of there to be.**
1. _____There was_____ a river at the end of this street 20 years ago.
2. _____ a park near here when you were young?
3. He said that _____ some cookies left.
4. _____ many people at the concert last week?
5. How many students _____ in the classroom yesterday?

3 **Complete the sentences with the future forms of there to be.**
1. How many girls _____will there be_____ at the meeting?
2. I believe _____ many, just you and me.
3. _____ enough sandwiches. I'll make some more.
4. _____ a person waiting for you at the airport.
5. _____ peace around the world in the future?

4 **Answer the questions.**
1. How many people are there in your house/ family?

2. Were there many children in the family five years ago?

3. Is there a special place in the world you want to know?

4. Was there a person in your life or family that you miss a lot?

5. Will there be peace around the world in ten years?

81 Verb Tense Table

	Present	Past	Future
Simple	v.[1] (+s/es) He often **cooks**. He **arrives** at 5:00.	v. (+d/ed) He **cooked** yesterday. He **swam** last week.	will + v. He **will cook** tomorrow.
	hábitos, fatos, verdades gerais; ação futura agendada	ação passada e finalizada em tempo definido.	ação futura
Progressive be + v.-ing	(am/is/are cooking) He **is cooking** now.	(was/were cooking) He **was cooking** when I arrived.	(will be cooking) He **will be cooking** at 4:00.
	ação em andamento no momento	ação em andamento no passado	ação em andamento no futuro
Perfect have + v.pp	(has/have cooked) He **has** never **cooked** dinner.[2]	(had cooked) He **had cooked** lunch when I arrived.	(will have cooked) He **will have cooked** lunch before noon.
	ação passada em tempo indefinido; ação que se iniciou no passado e que continua no presente	ação finalizada antes de outra no passado.	ação que terá terminado em determinado momento no futuro
Perfect Progressive have been + v. -ing	(has/have been cooking) He **has been cooking** for hours.	(had been cooking) He **had been cooking** for hours before I arrived.	(will have been cooking) He **will have been cooking** for hours before I get there.
	enfatiza a ação	enfatiza a ação	enfatiza a ação

Notes – **(1) Abreviations:** v. = verb pp = past participle; **(2) Traduções (a) Perfect Tenses:** Ele nunca fez o jantar; Ele tinha feito o almoço quando cheguei; Ele terá feito o almoço antes das 12:00; **(b) Perfect Progressive:** Ele está cozinhando há horas; Ele tinha cozinhado por horas antes que eu chegasse; Ele terá cozinhado por horas antes que eu chegue.

Exercises [answers on p. 215]

1 Choose the correct alternative.

1. She ___*has been*___ ill since Monday.
   a. have been   b. has been ✓   c. will have been
2. He _____ breakfast before I left home this morning.
   a. has had   b. will have   c. had had
3. Dinner _____ ready in five minutes.
   a. will be   b. does   c. doesn't
4. He _____ many questions last class.
   a. asked   b. asks   c. will ask
5. What _____ you _____ lately?
   a. have – done   b. had – done   c. will – done
6. What _____ on the other side of the street? Can you see it?
   a. is happening   b. was happening   c. will be happening
7. She _____ in that office last month.
   a. worked   b. works   c. is working
8. I _____ at the baby when he smiled.
   a. am looking   b. won't be looking   c. was looking
9. She's Italian, she _____ from Milan.
   a. don't come   b. comes   c. was
10. When you arrived I _____ for hours.
    a. have waited   b. will wait   c. had been waiting

2 Complete the sentence with the correct tense of the verbs given.

1. (see) I ___*'ll see*___ you tomorrow after class.
2. (lose) She _____ her keys when she went out last night.
3. (prepare) Yesterday I _____ lunch when he arrived.
4. (take) _____ you _____ many pictures recently?
5. (do) What _____ you _____ next month?
6. (fly) The birds _____ south now.
7. (buy) They _____ their books before I arrived.
8. (be) Next month they _____ together for ten years.
9. (have) We _____ dinner when the kids started laughing.
10. (finish) I _____ my homework in an hour.

82 Wh- questions

Palavras como **what**, **who**, **which**, **when** etc. podem ser usadas na formulação de perguntas. São geralmente seguidas por verbos auxiliares ou modais.

what (que, qual)	**What** do you like? **What** is your name?
which (qual = escolha restrita)	**Which** hand did you hurt? **Which** book is yours: this or that?
who (quem)	**Who** did you invite? **Who** can help us?
why (por que)	**Why** are they sad?
when (quando)	**When** did he arrive?
where (onde)	**Where** do you live?
whose (de quem)	**Whose** car did you drive?

Note – **What** é usado em perguntas genéricas; **Which** é usado quando a escolha é restrita: What plays did you see last year?, Which (of the plays) did you like best? [ver também How & Compounds p. 81]

Não se usa verbo auxiliar quando a palavra interrogativa é sujeito do verbo. Observe:

Who invited her? **Who** did she invite?
What happened? **What** did he say?
(subj.) (obj.)

Exercises [answers on p. 215]

1 Match the columns.

1. Whose keys are these? ____ a. They arrived in the morning.
2. Why are you happy? ____ b. She's the new director.
3. Which car do you prefer? ____ c. Because it's my birthday.
4. When did they arrive? ____ d. I prefer the black one.
5. Who is she? ____ e. On the second floor.
6. Where is the lab? _a_ f. They're mine.

2 Check the correct alternative.

1. a. Which of them is your sister? ✓
   b. Who of them is your sister?
2. a. What did happen?
   b. What happened?
3. a. What is your name: Sue or Helen?
   b. Which is your name: Sue or Helen?
4. a. Who bike is that?
   b. Whose bike is that?
5. a. Who did say that?
   b. Who said that?
6. a. Where you live?
   b. Where do you live?
7. a. Who did you meet?
   b. Who you meet?
8. a. Who does care?
   b. Who does she care about?

3 Ask questions about the underlined words.

1. The test is next Monday.
   When is the test?
2. Mr. Robertson's dog died.

3. He left because he was tired.

4. I saw a terrible accident.

5. One of the boys wrote the letter.

6. An old man fell in the river.

7. Her new house is near the park.

8. I live on the left side of the road.

83 X-doubts

Mixed doubts	
1. like, as (= como) **like** (semelhante a) He worked **like** a beaver. She runs **like** a gazelle. **as** (na **função** de) John works **as** a teacher. I've worked **as** a waiter in Rio.	**2. it takes/ took/ will take** (= leva, levou, levará) Expressam período de tempo: **It takes** ten minutes to get there. **It took** us one day to paint the room. **It will take** a day to finish the job.
3. whom (= quem, que) usado como objeto de verbo ou de preposição. To **whom** did you talk? **Whom** did you talk to? **Who** did you talk to?	**4. would rather, had better** **had better** (= é melhor) You**'d better** study harder. He**'d better** stay home. **would rather** (indica preferência) I**'d rather** stay home. She**'d rather** take a taxi.
5. enough (= suficiente) **antes de substantivos:** I have **enough** money. There is **enough** salt. There isn't **enough** time. **após adjetivos, verbos e advérbios:** He is tall **enough**. He runs fast **enough**. He arrived soon **enough**.	**6. each other, one another** (= um ao outro/uns aos outros) Na maioria das vezes podem ser usados no lugar um do outro. He and I saw **each other** here. The students helped **one another**. **One another** é mais usado na referência a mais de dois itens.

7. also, too, either
(= também)
also – em frase afirmativa; após **to be**, antes do verbo principal.
I **also** sing.
He **also** loves you.
Rita is **also** a singer.

too – no final de frase não negativa.
I can speak French **too**.
She is Greek, is he Greek **too**?

either – no final de frase negativa.
He isn't a good friend **either**.
She isn't Mexican **either**.

8. inversão
(sujeito/objeto)
É usada como ênfase depois de palavras de sentido restritivo como: only, seldom, rarely, no sooner, never, neither, little etc.
Never has he arrived late.

auxiliares e verbos de movimento fazem a própria inversão:
Here is the fridge.
Out went the light.

alguns verbos usam o auxiliar do:
Rarely do you find such honest people.
Seldom do we talk in such room.

9. so...I; neither...I
Expressam concordância:
so...I (= ... também)
em frases afirmativas.
— I **am** tired. — So **am** I.
— He **sleep**s late. — So **do** I.
— I **ate** too much. — So **did** I.
— I've **cau**ght a cold. — So **have** I.

neither... I/nor... I (= ... também não)
em frases negativas
— I **am not** tired.
— Neither/Nor **am** I.
— He **didn't** cook dinner.
— Neither/ Nor **did** she.
— I **haven't** had a promotion.
— Neither **have** I.

10. yet, already, still
yet (= ainda)
usado em perguntas e negativas:
Have you finished your homework **yet**?
I haven't finished it **yet**.
The apples are not ripe **yet**.

still (= ainda)
usado em negativas; antes de verbo mas após to be.
Are you **still** working at the office?
He was **still** asleep.
The bus **still** hasn't come.
I **still** don't know the answer.
You **still** love me.

already (= já)
usado em afimativas e interrogativas
The train has **already** left!
I have **already** finished.
Have you **already** finished?

84 Yes-no Questions

Yes/no questions são perguntas que demandam apenas *yes* ou *no* como resposta. São feitas por meio dos auxiliares e auxiliares modais (**be, do have, will, would, can, should** etc.) e sem o uso de palavras como *how, what, when* etc. Há diferentes respostas possíveis:

– Is he late?   – Yes, **he is late.**   – Yes, **he is.**   – Yes.
               – No, **he is not late.** – No, **he isn't.** – No.   – I don't know.

Observe as mais usuais.

Yes-no question	answers	
Are you Italian?	Yes, I **am**.	No, I**'m not**.
Are they busy?	Yes, they **are**.	No, they **aren't**.
Are they jogging?	Yes, they **are**.	No, they **aren't**.
Is he tired?	Yes, he **is**.	No, he **isn't**.
Is he going to run?	Yes, he **is**.	No, he **isn't**.
Was he busy?	Yes, he **was**.	No, he **wasn't**.
Were you late?	Yes, I **was**.	No, I **wasn't**.
Were they jogging?	Yes, they **were**.	No, they **weren't**
Do you work?	Yes, I **do**.	No, I **don't**.
Does he work?	Yes, he **does**.	No, he **doesn't**.
Did he study?	Yes, he **did**.	No, he **didn't**.
Has he arrived?	Yes, he **has**.	No, he **hasn't**.
Have you cried?	Yes, I **have**.	No, I **haven't**.
Had he left?	Yes, he **had**.	No, he **hadn't**.
Will they come?	Yes, they **will**.	No, they **won't**.
Would you help?	Yes, I **would**.	No, I **wouldn't**.
Can you swim?	Yes, I **can**.	No, I **can't**.
Could you sleep?	Yes, I **could**.	No, I **couldn't**.
May we go?	Yes, you **may**.	No, you **may not**.
Might he help?	Yes, he **might**.	No, he **mightn't**.
Should we go?	Yes, we **should**.	No, we **shouldn't**.

Exercises [answers on p. 216]

1 Answer the questions. Follow the example.

1. Are you my friend? — Yes, *I am.*
2. Was her dog in the garden? — Yes, _____
3. Are you going with us? — No, _____
4. Is this a good hotel? — Yes, _____
5. Were his friends nice people? — No, _____
6. Am I at the correct site? — No, _____
7. Was she working at 5? — No, _____
8. Is it raining? — No, _____
9. Was it snowing an hour ago? — Yes, _____
10. Is she working now? — Yes, _____
11. Was he studying? — Yes, _____
12. Were Tom and Jill at home? — Yes, _____

2 Answer the questions. Follow the example.

1. Do they smoke? — Yes, *they do.*
2. Do you like tea? — Yes, _____
3. Did he pass the examination? — No, _____
4. Does she arrive for lunch? — No, _____
5. Can we stay here? — Yes, _____
6. Could he study here? — No, _____
7. Should he write a message? — Yes, _____
8. Will they be here tomorrow? — No, _____
9. Would they get hurt? — Yes, _____
10. Has your brother left? — No, _____
11. Have they already gone? — Yes, _____
12. Had he left when you arrived? — Yes, _____

85 Zero Article

O artigo **The** é omitido:

1. com nomes de:

refeições:	breakfast	lunch	dinner
partes do dia:	at night	at midday	at noon
certos locais:	at school	at home	at work
dias:	Sunday	Monday	Friday
meses:	May	June	July
anos:	2025	1500	1888
estações:	winter	summer	spring
festividades:	New Year	Easter	Mother's Day
próprios:	Mary	Alan	Mr. Brown
continentes:	Africa	America	Europe
países (sing.):	Italy	India	France
cidades:	Rome	Delhi	Paris
ruas:	Oxford	Sunset	Oregon
idiomas:	Japanese	Italian	English
montanhas (sing.):	K2	Everest	Mount Blanc
aeroportos:	Kennedy	Saigon	Galeão
jogos:	footbal	soccer	tennis
revistas:	Time	Autoweek	Fortune

2. locais como home, church, school, hospital, prison, sea, work, bed etc. quando usados para o propósito original.

I go to **school** (to study).
I went to **church** (to pray).

mas, para outros propósitos:
I go to **the school** to paint the wall.

3. ao falarmos sobre coisas em geral

I hate **cheese**.
Soccer is very popular in Brazil.

mas, ao sermos específicos:
The soccer played in Brazil is incredible.

Exercises [answers on p. 216]

1 **Check the correct sentences.**

1. Do you like cheese? _✓_
2. He adores the cakes. ____
3. Pass me the cheese please! ____
4. I went to the church to meet a friend. ____
5. Education should be priority in Brazil. ____
6. The education we had was based on respect. ____
7. The cake you mother made was delicious. ____
8. The cheese I ate in your house was delicious. ____
9. Did they play the soccer yesterday? ____

2 **Check the correct sentences.**

1. People lack love and respect in our times. _✓_
2. The people who respect themselves respect others. ____
3. Mother was in the church and father at sea. ____
4. I am going to climb the Mount Everest this year. ____
5. Grandfather came to the breakfast. ____
6. I always have lunch at school and dinner at home. ____
7. I went to school but left my books at home. ____
8. I am from Brazil but I speak the English. ____
9. She's going to bed because it's late. ____

3 **Write The where needed.**

1. We left ____—____ Rome early, soon after ____—____ breakfast.
2. She is learning _____ Greek at _____ university.
3. I'll take you to _____ airport, to _____ Kennedy airport.
4. He was sent to _____ prison a year ago.
5. Do you like _____ pastrami?
6. _____ blue cheese in my favorite.
7. They go to _____ church on Sundays.
8. I left John at _____ school.
9. I went to the club to play _____ tennis.

178 | Z

Answers

1 Abstract Nouns I: characteristics

1. Check the correct synonyms for the abstract nouns below.

1. b;
2. c;
3. b;
4. a;
5. a;
6. b;
7. a;
8. b;
9. a;
10. a

2. Underline the correct words to complete the sentences.

1. pride;
2. affection;
3. love;
4. satisfaction;
5. hope;
6. decisions;
7. hunger;
8. joy;
9. freedom;
10. courage;
11. Time;
12. Creativity, mistakes

3. Underline the abstract nouns in each sentence.

1. truth;
2. Honesty, policy;
3. beauty;
4. cruelty;
5. advice;
6. idea, problem;
7. peace;
8. hatred;
9. lie;
10. pain;
11. Adversity;
12. justice

2 Abstract Nouns II: form

1. Underline the suffixes in the abstract nouns below.

1. affec*tion*;
2. agree*ment*;
3. ambi*tion*;
4. bruta*lity*;
5. careless*ness*;
6. cheerful*ness*;
7. communica*tion*;
8. confid*ence*;
9. crea*tion*;
10. curios*ity*;
11. dedica*tion*;
12. dictator*ship*;
13. disappoint*ment*;
14. disturb*ance*;
15. eager*ness*

2. Underline the prefixes in the abstract nouns below.

1. *dis*appointment;
2. *un*balance;
3. *in*formality;
4. *mis*calculation;
5. *in*utility;
6. *dis*approval;
7. *un*fair;
8. *mis*direction;
9. *mal*nutrition;
10. *mis*fortune;
11. *un*happiness;
12. *dis*advantage;
13. *dis*belief;
14. *in*difference;
15. *mal*administration

3. **Check the correct form of the corresponding abstract noun.**

1. b;	3. b;	5. a;	7. a;	9. a;
2. b;	4. b;	6. b;	8. a;	10. b

4. **Turn the words into abstract nouns. Use suffixes or prefixes.**

1. enjoyment;
2. fascination;
3. favoritism;
4. formality;
5. friendship;
6. gladness;
7. happiness;
8. heroism;
9. imagination;
10. movement
11. patriotism;
12. (dis)organization

3 Adjectives I: use

1. **Check the opposites of the underlined adjectives.**

1. c;	3. a;	5. c;	7. c;	9. a;
2. a;	4. c;	6. b;	8. b;	10. b

2. **Circle the correct adjective.**

1. black;
2. happy;
3. interesting;
4. strong;
5. intelligent;
6. old;
7. good;
8. yellow;
9. red;
10. blue and yellow

3. **Complete the sentences with the words in the box.**

1. interesting;
2. difficult;
3. new;
4. young;
5. Old;
6. brave;
7. careful;
8. good;
9. horrible;
10. delicious

4 Adjectives II: form

1. **Underline the correct words to complete the sentences.**

1. long;
2. frightened;
3. horse race;
4. powerless;
5. bored;
6. love story;
7. well-behaved;
8. wedding dress;
9. impossible;
10. interested

2. **Turn the words below into adjectives. Use suffixes (-ed, -ing, -y, -ful, -less, -ish, -able).**

1. angry;
2. beautiful;
3. childish/childless;
4. colorful/colorless;
5. disappointed/disappointing;
6. disgusted/disgusting;
7. drinkable/drinking;
8. easy;
9. excited / exciting;
10. fascinated / fascinating
11. foolish;
12. happy;
13. homeless;
14. hopeful/hopeless;
15. juicy;
16. lucky;
17. miserable;
18. painless/painful;
19. questionable;
20. ugly

5 Adjectives III: order

1. **Underline the correct order.**

   1. small white house;
   2. five good books;
   3. an old traveling salesman;
   4. first cold days;
   5. last two months;
   6. old dilapidated brick houses;
   7. small, dark brown, leather case;
   8. three empty houses;
   9. a big, dark-haired man

2. **Underline the correct order.**

   1. a singing international star;
   2. fresh British ingredients;
   3. an interesting, old Dutch man;
   4. an expensive, big German car;
   5. fine, old Spanish wine;
   6. an old white brick house;
   7. a wonderful old Italian clock;
   8. big, old, black dog;
   9. large, prehistoric animal bones;

6 Adverbs I : order

1. **Classify the underlined words as M, P, T, F, D (manner, place, time, frequency, doubt / degree).**

   1. D;
   2. M;
   3. M;
   4. P;
   5. F;
   6. T;
   7. F;
   8. T;
   9. D;
   10. D;
   11. D;
   12. P

2. Choose the correct words to complete the sentences.

1. c;
2. a;
3. b;
4. b;
5. a;
6. c;
7. c;
8. c;
9. a;
10. a

7 Adverbs II: form & spelling

1. Transform the adjectives below into adverbs.

1. gently;
2. simply;
3. loudly;
4. happily;
5. basically;
6. angrily;
7. terribly;
8. boringly;
9. carefully;
10. probably

2. Complete the sentences using adverbs.

1. quickly;
2. beautifully;
3. relatively;
4. nicely;
5. dramatically;
6. easily;
7. happily;
8. slowly;
9. poorly;
10. carefully

3. Check the correct words to complete the sentences.

1. b;
2. a;
3. a;
4. a;
5. a;
6. b;
7. a;
8. a.

8 Adverbs III: position

1. Underline the correct answer.

1. carefully;
2. well;
3. rarely;
4. there;
5. respectfully;
6. as soon as possible;
7. Tomorrow;
8. in summer;
9. seldom;
10. usually

2. Rewrite the words in parentheses in the correct place.

1. He drives fast;
2. We went to the club yesterday;
3. I arrived in there December;
4. I'm going to Japan next year;
5. Yes, I can easily open that can;
6. Yes, he is really handsome;
7. Badly they behaved;
8. Unfortunately, they missed the bus;
9. We are leaving right now;
10. She left silently.

9 Adverbs IV: order

1. Rewrite the sentences and place the words in the correct position.
1. We arrived in Jamaica last week;
2. It is very windy this morning;
3. You studied very hard yesterday;
4. He went there in a hurry;
5. She closed the door very carefully;
6. She finished the last chapter very quickly at home yesterday;
7. I studied peacefully in the library yesterday.

2. Check the wrong sentences.
5. He quickly joined his group for dinner.
6. I could easily find the way to the park;
7. He was born in December, 2010;
10. I have lived in a brick house in Nebraska.

10 Adverb or Adjective?

1. Circle the adverbs and underline the adjectives.
1. The grizzly bear is a large predator;
2. He ran *fast* to catch the bus;
3. I will *always* remember them;
4. I get up *early*;
5. I caught the early bus;
6. The birth of gunpowder was accidental;
7. The cheetah runs *incredibly quickly*;
8. The general atmosphere at the meeting was great;
9. He lives *exceedingly far*;
10. The students' feedback was *extremely* positive.

2. Complete the sentences with words from the box. Use each word twice.

1. early;	3. deep;	5. low;	7. low;	9. long;
2. deep;	4. late;	6. long;	8. late;	10. Early

3. **Choose the correct form to complete the sentences.**

1. extremely;
2. softly;
3. hard
4. slowly;
5. surprisingly;
6. modern;
7. well;
8. poorly;
9. fantastic;
10. small

Obs.: o item 11 não necessita de respostas.

12 Agreement: subject & verb

1. **Underline the correct verb form.**

1. is;
2. are;
3. are;
4. is;
5. was;
6. is;
7. are;
8. is;
9. are;
10. is

2. **Underline the correct verb form.**

1. thinks;
2. are;
3. is;
4. is;
5. is;
6. agree;
7. is;
8. dislike;
9. feel;
10. is

3. **Underline the correct verb form.**

1. are;
2. have;
3. is going;
4. is;
5. are;
6. is;
7. is;
8. has;
9. is;
10. was

13 Articles: indefinite & definite

1. **Fill in the blanks with the correct indefinite article.**

1. an;
2. an;
3. a;
4. a;
5. an;
6. a;
7. an;
8. a;
9. a;
10. a

2. **Fill in the blanks with the definite article, if needed.**

1. He went to the British Islands on vacation;
2. Maria looked out the window;
3. We spend a week at the Hilton annually;
4. The employees are paid monthly;
5. The chair is badly made;
6. Jean plays the piano well;
7. The people were disappointed by the election results;
8. It was an honor to be invited to the ceremony;
9. He studied the sun, the moon and the movement of the stars;
10. South America is bordered on the west by the Pacific Ocean.

3. **Underline the correct answer.**

1. in England;
2. an English, a short;
3. the most famous;
4. *Murder at the Vicarage*;
5. the investigations;
6. the world's longest; *The Mousetrap*;
7. a murder, the West End;
8. a Scottish;
9. the detective;
10. a ship's surgeon, the SS Mayumba, a voyage, the West African

14 Auxiliary & Modal Verbs

1. **Classify the underlined words as A (for auxiliary verb) or O (for ordinary verb).**

1. A;	3. O;	5. O;	7. A;	9. O;
2. A;	4. O;	6. O;	8. A;	10. O

2. **Classify the underlined words as M (for modal verb) or O (for ordinary verb).**

1. O;	3. O;	5. M;	7. M;	9. M;
2. O;	4. M;	6. O;	8. O;	10. O

3. **Choose the correct alternative.**

1. Do, take, cause; 2. carry, put; 3. keep

15 Basic Sentence Patterns

1. **Circle SV or SVO to classify the sentence pattern.**

1. SV;	3. SVO;	5. SVO;	7. SV;	9. SV;
2. SVO;	4. SVO;	6. SV;	8. SVO;	10. SVO

2. **Circle SVC or SVOC to classify the sentence pattern.**

1. SVOC;	3. SVC;	5. SVC;	7. SVC;	9. SVC;
2. SVOC;	4. SVC;	6. SVOC;	8. SVOC;	10. SVOC

3. **Complete the sentences with the correct complement from the box.**

1. doctors;
2. drive;
3. mom;
4. open;
5. intelligent;
6. comfortable;
7. mad;
8. 'Woolly';
9. fixed;
10. French

16 Be: present & past

1. **Complete the sentences with the correct form of to be.**

1. is;
2. is;
3. were;
4. are;
5. was;
6. was;
7. are;
8. was;
9. were;
10. are

2. **Turn the sentences into the negative form.**

1. He was not a very intelligent man;
2. They were not late for the show;
3. The musician is not busy today;
4. Muse is not the name of a band;
5. I am not a good rock singer.

3. **Turn the sentences into the interrogative form.**

1. Is Lollapalooza an annual music festival?;
2. Were Tony Bennet and Frank Sinatra famous singers?;
3. Is the Sabiá-laranjeira the national bird of Brazil?/ Is the national bird of Brazil the Sabiá-laranjeira?;
4. Are jaguars and sea turtles endangered species?;
5. Was Castro Alves a famous poet?

17 Collective & Compound Nouns

1. **Complete the sentences with collectives from the box.**

1. crew;
2. pride;
3. pack;
4. archipelago;
5. herd;
6. litter;
7. herd;
8. bouquet;
9. pride

2. **Check the words that form compound nouns.**

1. a;
2. a;
3. c;
4. b;
5. b;
6. c;
7. a;
8. b;
9. c.

3. **Form new words with the words below.**

1. horse race, boat race;
2. bus station, train station;
3. tennis ball, tennis shoes;
4. moon light, honey moon;
5. clothes shop, underclothes

18 Conditional Sentences (if clauses): use

1. **Rewrite the sentences. Use the Simple Conditional.**

1. I would go to the club next week;
2. Would you work next Monday?;
3. He would not (wouldn't) come today;
4. The teachers would help us;
5. You wouldn't meet him.

2. **Rewrite the sentences. Use the Conditional Perfect.**

1. She would have lived in Japan;
2. They would have sold the car;
3. I wouldn't have left home;
4. Would you have bought a bike?;
5. Would they have taught us?

3. **Circle the correct meaning: P (possible), U (unlikely) or (I) impossible.**

1. U;
2. I;
3. P;
4. P;
5. I;
6. U;
7. P;
8. U;
9. I;
10. U

4. **Check the correct alternative.**

1. I will go;
2. would talk;
3. wouldn't have missed;
4. won't see;
5. would be;
6. would have stopped

19 Conditional Sentences II: verb tenses

1. Complete the sentences. Use the verbs given.

1. melts;
2. will accept;
3. will do;
4. take;
5. will come;
6. will break;
7. will get;
8. Will – help

2. Complete the sentences. Use the verbs given.

1. would come;
2. would be;
3. would reach;
4. would answer;
5. would go;
6. would stay;
7. would be;
8. Would – help

3. Complete the sentences. Use the verbs given.

1. would have done;
2. would have come;
3. wouldn't have made;
4. would have been;
5. would have told;
6. would have broken;
7. wouldn't have gone;
8. Would – have helped

4. Check the correct alternative.

1. a;
2. b;
3. c;
4. b;
5. a;
6. a;
7. c;
8. c

20 Conjunctions I: list

1. Underline the correct alternative.

1. or;
2. and;
3. and;
4. for;
5. so;
6. or;
7. but;
8. but also

2. Complete the sentences with words from the box.

1. for;
2. also;
3. both;
4. neither;
5. yet;
6. so;
7. both;
8. so

3. Check the wrong sentences and correct the mistakes.

1. but also > but;
5. but > and;
6. and > so

188 | Answers

21 Conjunctions II: list

1. Choose the correct alternative.

1. however;
2. therefore;
3. while;
4. because;
5. Once;
6. whenever;
7. As;
8. until

2. Check the correct sentences.

All sentences are correct.

22 Countable and Uncountable Nouns

1. Complete the sentences with words from the box

1. piece;
2. kilos;
3. bottles, pack;
4. pieces;
5. slice;
6. tubes;
7. cartons;
8. sheet

2. Underline the uncountable nouns.

1. water, bread;
2. money;
3. patience, love;
4. sand;
5. fire;
6. light;
7. gold;
8. luggage

3. Check the uncountable nouns in the lists below.

Todas são incontáveis exceto:
1. hour, box, pack;
2. pieces, school;
3. words, song;
4. bucket, bottle

23 Degrees of Comparison I: more/most..., ...-er/-est

1. Underline the correct alternative.

1. most active;
2. more attractive;
3. most brilliant;
4. more careful;
5. more courageous

Answers | 189

2. Write the comparative and superlative forms of the words below

1. short, shorter, shortest;
2. late, later, latest;
3. early, earlier, earliest;
4. narrow, narrower, narrowest;
5. wise, wiser, wisest;
6. soon, sooner, soonest;
7. angry, angrier, angriest;
8. big, bigger, biggest;
9. heavy, heavier, heaviest

3. Supply the correct form of the words given.

1. cleverer;
2. more slowly;
3. longest road;
4. prettier;
5. most popular;
6. more intelligent;
7. more beautiful;
8. most difficult;
9. hottest

24 Degrees of Comparison II: irregular comparison

1. Check the correct alternative.

1. a;
2. b;
3. c;
4. c;
5. b;
6. b;
7. a;
8. a

2. Match the columns.

1. c;
2. e;
3. a;
4. b;
5. d

3. Complete the sentences. Use the words given.

1. colder and colder;
2. worse and worse;
3. more and more difficult;
4. less and less;
5. more and more expensive

4. Complete the sentences. Use the words given.

1. the more;
2. the better;
3. the better;
4. the less;
5. the faster

25 Demonstratives and Distributives: this, that etc.

1. Underline the correct demonstrative.

1. this;
2. This, that;
3. those;
4. these;
5. This;
6. That;
7. Those;
8. These

2. Supply the correct form of to be.

1. is;
2. are;
3. are;
4. was;
5. were;
6. is;
7. was;

3. Turn into Portuguese.

1. Nenhum dos dois times vai vencer o campeonato;
2. Cada mão tem cinco dedos;
3. (Um dos dois) John ou Serge foi despedido.

4. Underline the correct verb tense.

1. is;
2. has;
3. leads;
4. lives;
5. makes;
6. has;
7. was;

26 Do: present & past

1. Answer the questions. Use short answers.

1. Yes, I do;
2. No, she doesn't;
3. No, they don't;
4. Yes, I did;
5. No, I didn't

2. Turn the sentences into the interrogative form.

1. Do you go to school in the morning?;
2. Does your/ my sister love pancakes?;
3. Do the boys walk the dog in the afternoon?;
4. Did your/ my brother paint the gate yesterday?;
5. Do the workers always do their job?

3. Turn the sentences into the negative form.

1. We don't walk to school;
2. Claudia doesn't go to work by bus;
3. They don't love science fiction;
4. The students didn't work a lot;
5. He didn't build a dog house.

4. Ask questions. Use the words given.

1. Where do they live?;
2. Who does the boy love?;
3. When does he study?;
4. What did Ann paint?;
5. Why did she go home?

27 Do & Make

1. **Write sentences. Use the words given.**

   Sugestões:
   1. Who can do me a favor?;
   2. The children are making a fire;
   3. Jeff is going to make an attempt;
   4. This car does 60 miles per hour;
   5. Dad is doing the dishes.

2. **Rewrite the words under the correct heading.**

   Make: make arrangements; make a choice; make a comment; make a difference; make an effort; make an excuse; make money; make friends; make a journey; make love; make a mess; make a noise; make a payment; make a plan; make a speech; make a suggestion; make a visit

   Do: do the cooking; do the shopping; do badly; do business; do good; do harm; do well; do one's best; do one's nails; do a work

28 Exclamatory Sentences & Other Sentence Types

1. **Classify the sentences as D (declarative), IMP (imperative), INT (interrogative) or E (exclamatory).**

   1. IMP;
   2. D;
   3. E;
   4. E;
   5. INT;
   6. E;
   7. D;
   8. IMP;
   9. INT;
   10. E

2. **Rewrite the sentences according to the instructions.**

   Sugestões:
   1. (INT) Is it a poetry contest?, (E) Wow, it's a poetry contest!;
   2. (IMP) Read that magazine article, please, (IN) Have you read that magazine article?;
   3. (E) What a long river it is!, (IN) Is it a long river?;
   4. (E) Wow! It is snowing!, (D) It is (not) snowing.

29 Future Tenses I: general table

1. **Answer the questions. Use the words given.**

   1. The sun will rise at 6:00 tomorrow;

2. The train departs in 10 minutes;
3. The meeting begins at 2:00;
4. In 2030 all students will have their own computers at school.;
5. No, they won't let me go with you;
6. She will come soon

2. Check the correct alternative.

1. a;
2. c;
3. b;
4. b;
5. c;
6. c

30 Future Tenses II: future simple & going to

1. Rewrite the sentences in the negative form.

1. I will not (won't) make dinner;
2. We will not meet the girls at school;
3. They are not going to arrive soon;
4. He is not going to spend his vacations in Rio.

2. Rewrite the sentences in the interrogative form.

1. Will it be easy to do that?;
2. Will you help your friends?;
3. Am I going to find a new job?;
4. Are we going to visit her soon?

3. Underline the correct alternative.

1. am going to;
2. will be;
3. am going to;
4. will;
5. is going to;
6. will

31 Future Tenses III: future progressive & future perfect

1. Supply the future progressive of the verbs given.

1. will be waiting;
2. will be sleeping;
3. will be arriving;
4. will be getting;
5. will be flying;
6. will be finishing;
7. will be studying;
8. will be reading

2. Supply the future perfect of the verbs given.

1. will have moved;
2. will have landed;
3. will have sold;
4. will have received;
5. will have written;
6. will have cleaned;
7. will have baked;
8. will have stopped

3. Answer the questions.

Sugestões:
1. I will be reading;
2. Yes, I will;
3. No, I won't;
4. Yes, I will;
5. I will have done my exercises.

4. Ask questions. Use the information in parenthesis.

1. What will they be studying / doing tomorrow at this time?;
2. What will you be cooking for dinner?;
3. When will Janet be arriving?;
4. What time will they have arrived?;
5. Where will he have slept?

32 Gender of Nouns

1. Complete the list below. Use words from the box.

1. bride;
2. poetess;
3. godmother;
4. hostess;
5. nun;
6. lady;
7. witch;
8. policewoman;
9. empress;
10. tigress;
11. daughter-in-law;
12. step-mother;
13. heroine;
14. cow

2. Check the masculine form of the underlined words.

1. b;
2. a;
3. a;
4. b;
5. a;
6. a;
7. c;

3. Check the words common to masculine and feminine gender.

artist; baby; candidate; child; leader; president; reporter; servant; student; teacher; uncle

33 Gerund I: gerund & present participle

1. Supply the gerund form of the verbs given.

1. waiting;
2. being;
3. seeing;
4. going;
5. painting;
6. exceeding;
7. writing;
8. Driving;
9. Stepping;
10. cooking

2. Supply the present participle of the verbs given.

1. relaxing;
2. making;
3. living;
4. running;
5. swimming;
6. lying;
7. singing;
8. burning;
9. smiling;
10. getting

3. Classify the underlined words as G (for Gerund) or P (for Present Participle).

1. G;
2. P;
3. P;
4. P;
5. P;
6. G;
7. G;
8. P;
9. G

Obs.: o item 34 não necessita de respostas.

35 Have I: present & past

1. Classify the underlined verbs as P (principal) or A (auxiliary).

1. P;
2. A;
3. P;
4. P;
5. P;
6. A;
7. P;
8. A;
9. A

2. Check the correct alternative.

1. c;
2. a;
3. a;
4. c;
5. b;
6. b;
7. c;
8. b;
9. a

36 Have II: causative form

1. Check the correct alternative.

1. c;
2. c;
3. a;
4. a;
5. b;
6. c;
7. b;
8. c

2. **Rewrite the sentences. Use causative forms.**

1. She has her shoes polished;
2. He had the garden watered;
3. He is having his car mended;
4. She was having her hair cut;
5. We will have the roof repaired;
6. I have had the windows cleaned;
7. He had had his clothes ironed;
8. He may have the box sent.

37 How & Compounds

1. **Match the columns.**

1. c;
2. g;
3. e;
4. f;
5. b;
6. d;
7. h;
8. a

2. **Complete the dialogs with words from the box.**

1. how fast;
2. how long;
3. how high;
4. how heavy;
5. how;
6. how deep;
7. how big;
8. how wide

3. **Answer the questions about yourself.**

1. I am ... years old;
2. I am ... meters tall;
3. I go to ... by car/ on foot;
4. I feel fine / terrible;

38 Imperative

1. **Write a command to each situation.**

1. Brush your teeth;
2. Wash your hands;
3. Let's eat something;
4. Let's not stay here;
5. Let's not leave now;
6. Water the flowers;
7. Don't open the window;
8. Write it down.

2. **Choose a command to each situation.**

1. Let's visit her!;
2. Do not disturb!;
3. Have some water;
4. Do some exercise;

5. Behave yourself!;
6. Keep calm;
7. Use mine!;
8. Take the first left.

3. **Use the imperative to complete the dialogs.**

   Sugestões:
   1. Go ahead. Turn the first right;
   2. Have another cup;
   3. Let's stay home!/Let's watch TV!;
   4. Yes. Don't make any noise./Keep silent;
   5. Let's take a walk

39 Indefinites I: some, any, no, none

1. **Check the correct alternative.**

   1. b;   3. a;   5. b;   7. a;
   2. c;   4. c;   6. a;   8. b

2. **Complete the sentences with the correct indefinites.**

   1. any;   3. no;   5. any;   7. some;
   2. any;   4. none;   6. any;   8. any

3. **Transform the sentences. Give them a positive meaning.**

   1. There is some money in my pocket;
   2. He has some shoes;
   3. She bought some books;
   4. We (always) drink some coffee;
   5. I (usually) buy some magazines;
   6. I arrived with some good news;
   7. She does some housework;
   8. I have some good ideas.

40 Indefinites II: compounds

1. **Underline the correct alternative.**

   1. anything;   4. anything;   7. something;
   2. Nobody;   5. somewhere;   8. nowhere
   3. anybody;   6. something;

2. **Complete the sentences. Use compounds of some and any.**

1. anybody/somebody;
2. somewhere;
3. anywhere;
4. Somebody;
5. anybody/anything;
6. something;
7. anything

3. **Complete the sentences. Use compounds of *no* and *any*.**

1. Nobody;
2. nothing;
3. anything;
4. anyone/anybody;
5. anything;
6. nothing;
7. anywhere

4. **Complete the sentences. Use some, any, no and compounds.**

1. anybody;
2. nobody;
3. anything;
4. some;
5. anywhere;
6. no/some;
7. Somebody

41 Infinitive I: characteristics

1. **Complete the sentences with words from the box.**

1. sing;
2. cook;
3. climb;
4. help;
5. stay;
6. run;
7. go;
8. fall

2. **Complete the sentences with words from the box.**

1. to open;
2. to run/to go;
3. to answer;
4. to go/to run;
5. to sing;
6. to arrive;
7. to start;
8. to see

3. **Check the correct alternative.**

1. b;
2. b;
3. a;
4. b;
5. c;
6. a;
7. a;
8. b

Obs.: o item 42 não necessita de respostas.

43 Linking Verbs

1. **Underline the correct linking verb to complete the sentence.**

1. tasted;
2. looked;
3. became;
4. Stay;
5. became;
6. looked;
7. felt;
8. felt;
9. appeared;
10. looked

2. Underline the linking verbs.
1. became;   3. grow;   5. xx;   7. xx;   9. xx;
2. felt;   4. smelled;   6. tasted; 8. looked; 10. xx

3. Classify the underlined verb as L (linking) or A (action verb).
1. A;   3. L;   5. A;   7. A;   9. A;
2. A;   4. A;   6. L;   8. A;   10. L

44 Modal Auxiliaries I: characteristics

1. Check the best answer.
1. a;   3. a;   5. a;   7. b;
2. b;   4. a;   6. a;   8. b

2. Match the columns.
1. d;   2. a;   3. c;   4. b;   5. e

3. Turn the sentences into the interrogative form.
1. May I see your driver's license?;
2. Will she drive the car?;
3. Could you help me move the sofa?;
4. Should he see a doctor?;
5. Must we talk to him?

45 Modal Auxiliaries II: meaning

1. Underline the meaning expressed by the modal verb.
1. possibility;   6. ability;   11. prohibition;
2. permission;   7. obligation;   12. deduction;
3. deduction;   8. deduction;   13. polite request;
4. deduction;   9. possibility; 14. intention;
5. ability;   10. advice;   15. advice

2. Check the sentence with a similar meaning.
1. a;   2. b;   3. a;   4. a;   5. a

46 Mood

1. **Classify the sentences as Ind (indicative), Imp (imperative) or S (subjunctive mood).**

   1. Imp;
   2. I;
   3. S;
   4. I;
   5. S;
   6. Imp;
   7. I;
   8. I;
   9. Imp;
   10. I

2. **Write a command to each situation.**

   1. Play the guitar, girls!;
   2. Read your book!;
   3. Cook dinner, Sheila!;
   4. Walk home, boys!;
   5. Don't shout, kids!

3. **Fill in the blanks. Use the verbs given.**

   1. study;
   2. play;
   3. begin;
   4. be;
   5. paint;
   6. guard/guarded;
   7. were;
   8. were;
   9. be;
   10. were

47 Nouns I: characteristics

1. **Classify the underlined nouns as C (concrete) or A (abstract).**

   1. C;
   2. A;
   3. A;
   4. A;
   5. A;
   6. C

2. **Underline the uncountable nouns.**

   1. milk;
   2. rice;
   3. gold;
   4. Love, life;
   5. bread;
   6. water

3. **Match the pairs according to their gender.**

   1. e;
   2. a;
   3. d;
   4. f;
   5. b;
   6. c

4. **Underline the correct alternative.**

   1. women;
   2. child;
   3. babies;
   4. knives;
   5. box;
   6. peaches

5. **Classify the underlined words as S (subject) or O (object).**

1. O;
2. S;
3. S;
4. O;
5. O;
6. S

48 Nouns II: form

1. **Match the columns and build compound nouns.**

1. f;
2. a;
3. h;
4. e;
5. b;
6. g;
7. d;
8. c

2. **Underline the verbs that can function as nouns. Then choose one to complete the sentence.**

1. access, comb/access;
2. box, dream/dream;
3. answer, face/face;
4. milk, name/name;
5. question, step/question;
6. hope, kiss/kiss;
7. race, paint/race;
8. walk, show/walk

3. **Add a suffix to the word given and complete the sentence.**

1. building;
2. winner;
3. exception;
4. Quietness;
5. friendship;
6. socialism;
7. treatment;
8. Honesty

Obs.: o item 49 não necessita de respostas.

50 One

1. **Underline the correct verb form.**

1. is;
2. gets;
3. are;
4. are;
5. Are;
6. has;
7. was;
8. is

2. **Write one in the correct place.**

1. I'm just one player on the team;
2. That is the one person she wanted to marry;
3. She's the one I like the best;
4. There is only one left;
5. Babies start to talk at one;

6. Have you got one?;
7. One Tom Olson talked to me;
8. Problems should come one at a time;
9. One can catch fine trout in this river;
10. You will see him one day.

3. Check the best translation.

1. a;   2. b;   3. a;   4. a;   5. b

51 Ordinary Verbs

1. Underline the main verbs in the following sentences.

1. was;   3. has;   5. does;   7. speak;   9. had;
2. waiting; 4. lived;   6. do;   8. swim;   10. have

2. Underline the correct alternative.

1. chooses;   5. speak;   8. liked;
2. like;   6. walked;   9. understands;
3. lives;   7. wrote;   10. wanted
4. talked;

3. Check the correct interrogative or negative form for the sentences below

1. a;   2. a;   3. b;   4. a;   5. b

52 Participles: present & past

1. Circle Pr (present) or Pt (past participle) to classify the underlined participle.

1. Pr;   3. Pr;   5. Pr;   7. Pt;   9. Pr;
2. Pt;   4. Pr;   6. Pt;   8. Pr;   10. Pt

2. Choose the correct participle to complete the sentence.

1. frightened;   4. depressing;   7. exciting;
2. exhausting;   5. depressed;   8. interesting;
3. bored;   6. fascinated;   9. frustrated

3. **Complete the sentences with words from the box.**

1. broken;
2. talking;
3. disappointed;
4. running;
5. wrecked;
6. repaired;
7. bored;
8. tired;
9. shocking

4. **Write the present and past participle of the following verbs.**

give – giving, given;
write – writing, written;
do – doing, done;
take – taking, taken;
speak – speaking, spoken;
fall – falling, fallen

53 Passive Voice

1. **Complete the sentences in the passive voice. Use the correct verb form.**

1. can be taken;
2. must be obeyed;
3. was broken;
4. will be given;
5. was eaten;
6. was being cleaned;
7. were written;
8. are paid

2. **Rewrite the sentences in the passive voice.**

1. The employees are paid;
2. The old brick house has been sold;
3. Your old bike had been brought;
4. Dinner would be cooked;
5. The gate near the old house is being painted;
6. The show has been canceled;
7. The car is going to be repaired;
8. Some tea has been dropped.

3. **Rewrite the two possible passive sentences.**

1. She will be given a gold ring. / A gold ring will be given to her.
2. We were told the truth. / The truth was told to us.
3. Ann was showed his new cars. / His new cars were shown to Ann.
4. Paul has been taught French. / French has been taught to Paul.
5. Ted was offered a new job. / A new job was offered to Ted.
6. I was sent a letter. / A letter was sent to me.

54 Past Tenses I: general table

1. Identify the types of action.

1. a;
2. c;
3. a;
4. b;
5. b;
6. c;
7. d;
8. a

2. Check the correct alternative.

1. b;
2. a;
3. b;
4. a;
5. c;
6. a;
7. a;
8. b

55 Past Tenses II: past progressive

1. Complete the sentences with the past progressive of the given verbs.

1. were sleeping;
2. was riding;
3. was cutting;
4. was studying, they were swimming;
5. was driving;
6. was lying;
7. were playing;
8. was winning

2. Match questions and answers.

1. c;
2. g;
3. b;
4. d;
5. a;
6. h;
7. f;
8. e

56 Past Tenses III: past simple – regular verbs

1. Write the past form of the verbs below.

1. liked;
2. cared;
3. admitted;
4. hurried;
5. talked;
6. preferred;
7. enjoyed;
8. planned;
9. studied;
10. robbed

2. Rewrite the sentences according to the information given.

1. Did he arrive late last night?;
2. We didn't play golf yesterday;
3. She didn't love him years ago;
4. Did you talk to the teacher?;
5. What did Paul study?;
6. Where did you hurry to?

3. **Complete the sentences with the past simple of the verbs given.**

1. rained;
2. stopped;
3. danced;
4. watched;
5. studied;
6. bake;
7. cook;
8. arrive

57 Past Tenses IV: past simple – irregular verbs

1. **Write the past form of the verbs below.**

1. took;
2. made;
3. did;
4. was, were;
5. had;
6. came;
7. put;
8. read;
9. taught;
10. bought

2. **Rewrite the sentences according to the information given.**

1. Did he come home late?;
2. We didn't swim yesterday;
3. She didn't leave him years ago;
4. What did Paul buy?;
5. Where did you go on Sunday?

3. **Check the correct alternative.**

1. c;
2. a;
3. c;
4. b;
5. c;
6. a;
7. c;
8. a

4. **Answer the questions about yourself.**

1. I went to…;
2. I saw…;
3. I left home at…;
4. I went back home at…

58 Past Tenses V: past perfect & past perfect progressive

1. **Rewrite the sentences using the information given.**

1. Had you read his books …;
2. The plane hadn't landed …;
3. Where had they been …;
4. Who had been waiting for Carol?;
5. What had she played …

2. **Complete the sentences with the past perfect of the verbs given.**

1. had left;
2. had finished;
3. had given;
4. had had;
5. had done;
6. had destroyed;
7. had lived;
8. had missed

3. **Underline the correct alternative.**

1. had hurt;
2. had been doing;
3. had left;
4. hadn't wun;
5. had been;
6. said;
7. left;
8. had been working

59 Personal Pronouns: subject & object

1. **Classify the underlined pronouns as: S (for subject) or O (for object).**

1. O;
2. S;
3. S;
4. S;
5. O;
6. S;
7. O;
8. O;
9. O;
10. S

2. **Underline the correct pronoun.**

1. I;
2. They;
3. us;
4. her;
5. you;
6. me;
7. them;
8. him;
9. me;
10. me

3. **Substitute the underlined words. Use pronouns.**

1. it;
2. them;
3. it;
4. He;
5. him;
6. us;
7. them;
8 them;
9. They, her

Obs.: o item 60 não necessita de respostas.

61 Plural of Nouns: regular & irregular

1. **Rewrite the words in the plural form.**

1. bushes;
2. cherries;
3. cliffs;
4. bosses;
5. beauties;
6. selves;
7. geese;
8. families;
9. donkeys;
10. children;
11. chimneys;
12. echoes;
13. feet;
14. diaries

2. **Underline the correct alternative.**

1. baby;
2. dresses;
3. strawberries;
4. mice;
5. feet;
6. sandwiches;
7. spoonfuls;
8. trousers

3. **Check the correct sentences. Correct the mistakes.**

Correct: 1, 4, 5, 8
Incorrect: 2. boxes; 3. glasses; 6. wishes; 7. flies

4. Rewrite the sentences in the plural form.

1. These old watches are lovely;
2. There are old churches around the parks;
3. We are sure they are good children;
4. Did the policemen arrest the thieves?;
5. Are there any knives in the drawers?;
6. They are going to tell us interesting stories.

62 Possessive Adjectives & Pronouns

1. Classify the underlined possessive as Adj (adjective) or Pr (pronoun).

1. Adj;
2. Adj;
3. Pr;
4. Pr;
5. Adj;
6. Pr;
7. Adj;
8. Pr;
9. Adj

2. Circle the correct alternative.

1. b;
2. a;
3. a;
4. c;
5. b;
6. c;
7. b;
8. a;
9. a

3. Complete the sentence with the correct possessive.

1. our;
2. his;
3. her;
4. My;
5. their;
6. their;
7. her;
8. Their;
9. His

63 Possessive of Nouns ('s or ')

1. Supply ['] or ['s].

1. The men's gloves;
2. The miners' boots;
3. The sheep's ears;
4. The hunter's hat;
5. The dogs' puppies;
6. My mother's sister;
7. The birds' nest;
8. Adam's apple;
9. The puppy's ears;
10. My father's voice;
11. The children's toys;
12. The doctor's smile;
13. The ladies' glasses;
14. The bears' trail;
15. Jesus' disciples;
16. Dennis'/'s room.

2. Write the sentences. Use ['] or ['s].

1. The kid's restroom;
2. A friend's car;
3. Gabriel's house;
4. The twins' names;
5. My dog's name;
6. The girls' cats;
7. The deer's trail;
8. Kat's shoes.

3. Supply ['] or ['s].

1. The soldiers';
2. the children's;
3. the Browns';
4. Jason's; Tania's;
5. The babies';
6. the doctor's;
7. The Smiths';
8. Whales'

64 Prefixes & Suffixes

1. Rewrite the words using the prefixes given.

1. interview, interrelated;
2. unavailable, unclear;
3. unnatural, untidy;
4. refill, replay;
5. disconnect, disappear;
6. incorrect, indifference;
7. deform, deforest;
8. transport, transocean;
9. misspell, mistake

2. Rewrite the words using the suffixes given.

1. careless, harmless;
2. fiercely, peacefully;
3. noisy, rainy;
4. doer, employer;
5. recyclable, drinkable;
6. darkness, laziness;
7. truthful, faithful;
8. painting, reading;
9. employment, movement

3. Add the correct prefix or suffix to the word given.

1. disagree;
2. unlock;
3. reopen;
4. Unpack;
5. useful;
6. usually;
7. interesting;
8. misspell;
9. singer;

Obs.: o item 65 não necessita de respostas.

66 Preposition Combinations: prepositions after verbs

1. Underline the correct preposition.

1. protected from;
2. learned about;
3. pointed at;
4. invited to;
5. prevent from;
6. infer from;
7. impressed on;
8. named after

2. Check the correct preposition.

1. c;
2. b;
3. c;
4. b;
5. a;
6. a;
7. a;
8. c;
9. c;
10. c

3. **Supply the correct preposition.**

1. run after;
2. trust in;
3. rely on;
4. vary from;
5. recovered from;
6. shout at;
7. shouted for;
8. protest against;
9. return to;
10. searched for

67 Present Tenses I: general table

1. **Identify the types of action.**

1. a;
2. d;
3. c;
4. b;
5. c;
6. a;
7. a;
8. e

2. **Check the correct alternative.**

1. a;
2. b;
3. a;
4. b;
5. b;
6. a;
7. c;
8. a

68 Present Tenses II: present progressive

1. **Write sentences in the present progressive. Use the words given.**

1. She is running in the park;
2. We are not beginning the exercise;
3. I am not doing the dishes;
4. Is Paul writing a song?;
5. The boy is not lying;
6. Are the children playing soccer?;
7. Are you riding a bike?;
8. Is the phone ringing?

2. **Complete the sentences with the present progressive of the verbs given.**

1. aren't swimming, are studying;
2. are lying;
3. Is – playing;
4. is – cutting;
5. is not ringing;
6. are writing;
7. are – studying;
8. Are – leaving

3. **Match questions and answers.**

1. f;
2. h;
3. a;
4. c;
5. d;
6. b;
7. g;
8. e

69 Present Tenses III: present simple

1. Rewrite the sentence according to the information given.

1. I don't work near my house;
2. Does John sleep early?;
3. They always get late;
4. Does he often wash his car?;
5. Sheila doesn't study French.

2. Supply the correct form of the verb given.

1. misses;
2. Does – rush;
3. goes;
4. catches;
5. doesn't brush

3. Underline the correct verb form.

1. speaks;
2. don't watch;
3. Does – stop;
4. doesn't dance;
5. do – live;
6. don't drive;
7. does – like;
8. drink

4. Answer the questions.

1. I go to (the)…;
2. I study in the…;
3. I go to school on foot/by…;
4. He/ She goes to school on foot/by…

70 Present Tenses IV: present perfect & past simple

1. Rewrite the sentences according to the information given.

1. I haven't seen David recently;
2. Has he studied Greek?;
3. Who have they talked to?;
4. Where have you lived?;
5. They have moved to Rio;
6. We have bought a house;
7. Has Julia come from Japan?;
8. We haven't had lunch at home.

2. Supply the present perfect tense of the verbs given.

1. have – written;
2. has worked;
3. have gone;
4. Have – been;
5. have – visited;
6. have not seen;
7. has lived;
8. have not arrived

3. Complete the sentences with the correct tense of the verbs given.

1. have been;
2. were;
3. has broken;
4. broke;
5. finished;
6. Have – finished;
7. bought;
8. have bought

71 Present Tenses V: present perfect & present perfect progressive

1. Turn into Portuguese.
   1. Você mentiu para mim muitas vezes;
   2. Viajamos/ temos viajado de trem ultimamente;
   3. James e Kate acabam de se mudar;

2. Rewrite the adverb in the correct place.
   1. I have met many people since I arrived;
   2. He has been sleeping well recently;
   3. We haven't seen Laura yet;
   4. Have you ever been to Petra?;
   5. He has never visited us;
   6. They have just got married;
   7. Has Linda already arrived?;
   8. I have seen that movie many times.

3. Check the correct alternative.

   1. a;   3. a;   5. b;   7. b;
   2. a;   4. c;   6. c;   8. b

72 Quantifiers: much, many etc.

1. Complete the sentences with much or many.
   1. many;   4. Many;   7. many;
   2. much;   5. many;   8. many
   3. much;   6. much;

2. Complete the sentences with or little or few.
   1. little;   4. few;   7. few;
   2. little;   5. little;   8. few
   3. few;   6. Few;

3. Check the correct alternative.
   1. b;   3. b;   5. c;   7. b;
   2. a;   4. c;   6. c;   8. b

Answers | 211

73 Questions: direct & indirect (embedded)

1. **Choose the correct indirect question.**
   1. a; 2. b; 3. a; 4. b; 5. b

2. **Complete the sentence to transform the question into indirect question.**
   1. why they moved to Brazil;
   2. how she has managed to get so rich;
   3. how much that skate costs;
   4. what time the plane landed;
   5. we could meet next Friday;
   6. where Oxford Street is;
   7. what she wanted;
   8. who arrived

74 Reflexive Pronouns

1. **Classify the underlined pronoun as R (reflexive), E (emphatic) or I (idiomatic).**
   1. R; 2. I; 3. E; 4. E; 5. R; 6. R; 7. E; 8. R

2. **Choose the correct alternative.**
   1. herself;
   2. himself;
   3. themselves;
   4. themselves;
   5. myself;
   6. yourself;
   7. itself;
   8. ourselves

3. **Supply the correct reflexive pronoun.**
   1. myself;
   2. herself;
   3. himself;
   4. ourselves;
   5. themselves;
   6. himself;
   7. themselves;
   8. herself

75 Relative Pronouns I: who, which, that etc.

1. **Classify the relative pronoun in the underlined sentence as S (subject) or O (object)**
   1. S; 2. S; 3. O; 4. S; 5. O; 6. S; 7. O; 8. S

2. Underline the correct pronouns to complete the sentences.

1. who;
2. whose;
3. that;
4. xx;
5. where;
6. xx;
7. whom;
8. that;
9. which;
10. which

3. Complete the sentences with all possible relative pronouns.

1. where, in which;
2. whose;
3. who, that, xxx;
4. which, that, xxx;
5. who, that;
6. which, that;
7. which, that, xxx;
8. whose;
9. who, that;
10. which, that

76 Relative Pronouns II: relative clauses

1. Classify the underlined clause as D (defining) or ND (non-defining).

1. D;
2. ND;
3. ND;
4. D;
5. ND;
6. ND;
7. ND;
8. D

2. Complete the sentences with all possible relative pronouns.

1. who, that;
2. who;
3. which;
4. who, that;
5. which, that, xxx;
6. which, that, xxx;
7. who, whom, that, xxx;
8. who;
9. whose;
10. who

3. Complete the sentences with all possible relative pronouns.

1. who;
2. which;
3. whose;
4. where;
5. which;
6. where;
7. which;
8. who;
9. who(m);
10. which

77 Reported (Indirect) Speech

1. Supply the correct verb tense.

1. had seen;
2. there was;
3. would see;
4. didn't know;
5. were happy;
6. could go;
7. had painted;
8. would sing;
9. had already been;
10. had invited

Answers | 213

2. **Rewrite the sentences. Use reported speech.**

1. what time I would be home;
2. She liked coffee;
3. me why he had left;
4. them to leave the room;
5. the baby had been laughing.

3. **Rewrite the sentences in the reported speech form.**

1. it is raining;
2. the earth moves round the sun;
3. honesty is the best policy;
4. the Hindus burn their dead.

Obs.: o item 78 não necessita de respostas.

79 Tag Question

1. **Check the correct tag question.**

1. c;
2. a;
3. a;
4. c;
5. a;
6. c;
7. a;
8. b;
9. c;
10. b

2. **Supply the correct tag questions.**

1. did she;
2. don't they;
3. hadn't we;
4. won't you;
5. have they;
6. shouldn't he;
7. weren't they;
8. shall we;
9. doesn't she;
10. isn't she

80 There to be: present & past

1. **Complete the sentences with the present forms of there to be.**

1. There is;
2. Is there;
3. There aren't;
4. Is there;
5. There are

2. **Complete the sentences with the past forms of there to be.**

1. There was;
2. Was there;
3. there were;
4. Were there;
5. were there

3. **Complete the sentences with the future form of there to be.**

1. will there be;
2. there won't be;
3. there won't be;
4. There will be;
5. Will there be

4. **Answer the questions.**

1. There are...;
2. Yes, there were / No, there weren't;
3. Yes, there is / No, there isn't;
4. Yes, there was/No, there wasn't;
5. Yes, there will be/No, there won't be.

81 Verb Tense Table

1. **Choose the correct alternative.**

1. b; 3. a; 5. a; 7. a; 9. b;
2. c; 4. a; 6. a; 8. c; 10. c

2. **Complete the sentence with the correct tense of the verbs given.**

1. will see;
2. lost;
3. was preparing;
4. Have – taken;
5. will – do;
6. are flying;
7. had bought;
8. will have been;
9. were having;
10. will finish

82 Wh-questions

1. **Match the columns.**

1. f; 3. d; 5. b;
2. c; 4. a; 6. e

2. **Check the correct alternative.**

1. a; 3. b; 5. b; 7. a;
2. b; 4. b; 6. b; 8. b

3. **Ask questions about the underlined words.**

1. When is the test?;
2. Whose dog died?;
3. Why did he leave?;
4. What did you see?;
5. Who wrote the letter?/Which of the boys wrote the letter?;
6. What happened?;
7. Where is her new house?;
8. On which side of the road do you live?

Obs.: o item 83 não necessita de respostas.

84 Yes-no Questions

1. Answer the questions. Follow the example.

1. Yes, I am;
2. Yes, it was;
3. No, I'm not;
4. Yes, it is;
5. No, they weren't;
6. No, you aren't;
7. No, she wasn't;
8. No, it isn't;
9. Yes, it was;
10. Yes, she is;
11. Yes, he was;
12. Yes, they were.

2. Answer the questions. Follow the example.

1. Yes, they do;
2. Yes, I do;
3. No, he didn't;
4. No, she doesn't;
5. Yes, you can;
6. No, he couldn't;
7. Yes, he should;
8. No, they won't;
9. Yes, they would;
10. No, he hasn't;
11. Yes, they have;
12. Yes, he had.

85 Zero Article

1. Check the correct sentences.

Correct: 1, 3, 4, 5, 6, 7, 8
Incorrect: 2, 9

2. He adores cakes;
9. Did they play soccer yesterday?

2. Check the correct sentences.

Correct: 1, 2, 6, 7, 9
Incorrect: 3, 4, 5, 8

3. Mother was in church and father at sea;
4. I am going to climb Mount Everest this year;
5. Grandfather came to breakfast;
8. I am from Brazil but I speak English.

3. Write The where needed.

1. We left Rome early, soon after breakfast;
2. She is learning Greek at university;
3. I'll take you to the airport, to Kennedy airport;
4. He was sent to prison a year ago;
5. Do you like pastrami?;
6. The blue cheese in my favorite;
7. They go to church on Sundays;
8. I left John at school;
9. I went to the club to play tennis.

Irregular Verbs

base form	past tense	past participle	translation
arise	arose	arisen	surgir
awake	awoke	awoken	acordar
be	was/were	been	ser/estar
bear	bore	born	suportar
beat	beat	beaten	bater
become	became	become	tornar-se
begin	began	begun	começar
behold	beheld	beheld	observar
bend	bent	bent	curvar
bet	bet	bet	apostar
bit	bid	bid/bidden	ordenar
bind	bound	bound	atar
bite	bit	bitten	morder
bleed	bled	bled	sangrar
blow	blew	blown	soprar
break	broke	broken	quebrar
breed	bred	bred	criar
bring	brought	brought	trazer
build	built	buit	construir
burn	burned/burnt	burned/burnt	queimar
burst	burst	burst	explodir
bust	bust	bust	estourar
buy	bought	bought	comprar
cast	cast	cast	arremessar
catch	caught	caught	pegar
choose	chose	choosen	escolher
clap	clapped/clapt	clapped/clapt	aplaudir
cling	clung	clung	agarrar
come	came	come	vir
cost	cost	cost	custar
creep	crept	crept	rastejar
cut	cut	cut	cortar
deal	dealt	dealt	tratar

base form	past tense	past participle	translation
dig	dug	dug	cavar
dive	dived/dove	dived	mergulhar
do	did	done	fazer
draw	drew	drawn	desenhar
dream	dreamed/dreamt	dreamed/ dreamt	sonhar
drink	drank	drunk	beber
dwell	dwelled/dwelt	dwelled/dwelt	habitar
eat	ate	eaten	comer
fall	fell	fallen	cair
feed	fed	fed	alimentar
feel	felt	felt	sentir
fight	fought	fought	lutar
find	found	found	achar
fit	fitted/fit	fitted/fit	adaptar
flee	fled	fled	fugir
fling	flung	flung	arremessar
fly	flew	flown	voar
forbid	forbade	forbidden	proibir
forget	forgot	forgotten	esquecer
freeze	froze	frozen	congelar
get	got	gotten	conseguir
give	gave	given	dar
go	went	gone	ir
grind	ground	ground	moer
grow	grew	grown	crescer
hang	hung	hung	pendurar
have	had	had	ter
hear	heard	heard	ouvir
hide	hid	hid /hidden	esquecer
hit	hit	hit	bater
hold	held	held	segurar
hurt	hurt	hurt	ferir
keep	kept	kept	manter
kneel	kneeled/knelt	kneeled/knelt	ajoelhar-se
knit	knitted/knit	knitted/knit	tricotar
know	knew	known	saber
lay	laid	laid	pôr

base form	past tense	past participle	translation
lead	led	led	conduzir
lean	leaned/leant	leaned/leant	inclinar
leap	leapt	leapt	pular
learn	learned/learnt	learned/learnt	aprender
leave	left	left	sair
lend	lent	lent	emprestar
let	let	let	deixar
lie	lay	lain	deitar-se; situar
light	lighted/lit	lighted/lit	acender
lose	lost	lost	perder
make	made	made	fazer
mean	mean	meant	significar
meet	met	met	encontrar
mow	mowed	mowed/mown	aparar
pay	paid	paid	pagar
put	put	put	pôr
quit	quitted/quit	quitted/quit	desistir
read	red	red	ler
rid	rid	rid	libertar
ride	rode	ridden	andar de
ring	rang	rung	tocar; soar
rise	rose	risen	levantar-se
run	ran	run	correr
saw	sawed	sawed/sawn	serrar
say	said	said	dizer
see	saw	seen	ver
seek	sought	sought	procurar
sell	sold	sold	vender
send	sent	sent	enviar
set	set	set	pôr
sew	sewed	sewed/sewn	costurar
shake	shook	shaken	agitar
shed	shed	shed	abrigar
shine	shone	shone	brilhar
shoe	shod	shod	calçar
shoot	shot	shot	atirar
show	showed	showed/shown	mostrar

base form	past tense	past participle	translation
shrink	shrank	shrunk	encolher
shut	shut	shut	fechar
sing	sang	sung	cantar
sink	sank	sunk	afundar
sit	sat	sat	sentar
sleep	slept	slept	dormir
slide	slid	slid	deslizar
smell	smelled/smelt	smelled/smelt	cheirar
sneak	sneaked/snuck	sneaked/snuck	andar furtivamente
sow	sowed	sowed/sown	semear
speak	spoke	spoken	falar
speed	speeded/sped	speeded/sped	correr
spell	spelled/spelt	spelled/spelt	soletrar
spend	spent	spent	gastar
spill	spilled/spilt	spilled/spilt	derramar
spin	span	spun	fiar; girar
spit	spit/spat	spit/spat	cuspir
split	split	split	dividir
spoil	spoiled/spoit	spoiled/spoilt	estragar
spread	spread	spread	espalhar
spring	sprang	sprung	saltar
stand	stood	stood	permanecer
steal	stole	stolen	roubar
stick	stuck	stuck	grudar
sting	stung	stung	picar
stink	stank	stunk	cheirar mal
strike	struck	struck	golpear
string	strung	strung	enfileirar; amarrar
strip	stripped/strip	stripped/strip	desnudar
strive	strove	striven	esforçar-se
swear	swore	sworn	jurar
sweat	sweated/sweat	sweated/sweat	transpirar
sweep	swept	swept	varrer
swell	swelled	swelled/swollen	inchar
swim	swam	swum	nadar
swing	swung	swung	balançar
take	took	taken	tomar

base form	past tense	past participle	translation
teach	taught	taught	ensinar
tear	tore	torn	rasgar
tell	told	told	contar
think	thought	thought	pensar
throw	threw	thrown	atirar
tread	trod	trodden	marchar
undergo	underwent	undergone	aguentar
understand	understood	understood	entender
wake	waked/woke	waked/woken	acordar
wear	wore	worn	vestir
wed	wed	wed	casar(-se)
weep	wept	wept	chorar
wet	wetted/wet	wetted/wet	molhar
win	won	won	vencer
wind	wound	wound	dar corda
withdraw	withdrew	withdrawn	retrair
withhold	withheld	withheld	reter
withstand	withstood	withstood	resistir; opor-se
write	wrote	written	escrever

Conheça também:

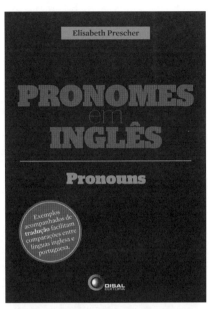

www.disaleditora.com.br

Este livro foi composto nas fontes Gotham e The Antiqua B e
impresso em janeiro de 2019 pela Paym Gráfica Editora Ltda.,
sobre papel offset 75g/m².